$6.95

NOTHING LEFT TO LOSE

STUDIES OF STREET PEOPLE

by Jeffrey D. Blum and Judith E. Smith

A SANCTUARY BOOK

"*Nothing Left to Lose* is an excellent and often moving account of the encounter between counselor and client in a paraprofessional counseling center. The lives of individuals in this book and the creative ways in which the counselors responded to their crises illustrate the stresses and strengths of the culture emerging in American society."—Philip Slater

Nothing Left to Lose challenges the myths that surround street people, with detailed case studies of thirty-three youths who sought help at Sanctuary, a hostel and counseling center in Cambridge, Massachusetts. Besides illustrating the major problems of street life, the book describes a unique, experimental counseling technique developed by the sympathetic young Sanctuary staff, who shared their clients' disillusionment with prevailing American values.

Sanctuary began in the summer of 1970 when thousands of runaway youths poured into Cambridge, eager to compare distant impressions of hip life with the real thing on Cambridge Common. Finding little that met with their expectations, they became lost in a shuffle of drugs, sex, and the aimless and wasteful aspects of street life. Some returned home; some "made it" as street people; others found themselves in terrible emotional crises, in prisons or mental hospitals.

SE

eet people dis-
tween the ages
one third are
m working-class
mes.
make the store-
es where authen-
lop," Smith and
rs try to be honest
s much as they try
ids' emotions. . . ."
hould be read by
the problems of
the sickness of
d be of immense
sel youth.

uated from Har-
Radcliffe, in 1970.
d with Sanctuary:
ffrey as assistant

Freedom's just another word for nothin' left to lose
by Kris Kristofferson and Fred Foster

NOTHING LEFT TO LOSE

Studies of Street People

JEFFREY D. BLUM/JUDITH E. SMITH

A Sanctuary Book

BEACON PRESS BOSTON

Library of Congress catalog card number: 72-75545
Published simultaneously in hardcover and paperback editions
International Standard Book Numbers: 0-8070-2584-4 (hardcover)
0-8070-2585-2 (paperback)
Beacon Press books are published under the auspices of
the Unitarian Universalist Association
Published simultaneously in Canada by Saunders of Toronto, Ltd.

Printed in the United States of America

To the young people
and counselors in this book
and to each other

Contents

PREFACE

During the summer of 1970, more than thirty thousand transients–some street people, some vacationing college students–spent time digging the hip scene in the Boston area, especially on the Boston Common and in the Harvard Square section of Cambridge, a long-time mecca for the young. In July 1970, The Sanctuary, founded by two students at the Episcopal Theological School, set up a storefront counseling center, a hotline, and a hostel on Mount Auburn Street a few blocks from the center of Harvard Square. During that summer the hostel provided free food and shelter for twenty-seven hundred kids for an average of two nights each. Sanctuary counselors participated in about 140 "serious" relationships with kids, some lasting for just a few intense days, others continuing into the fall, and a handful still going on today, almost a year later.

This book presents case studies of thirty-three of these individuals and the questions they faced, as well as a discussion of the counseling they received at Sanctuary. The cases include twelve females and twenty-one males. Twenty-six fall between the ages of thirteen and nineteen, and the remaining seven are in their early twenties. Approximately one-third of the cases are about blacks, reflecting the proportion of blacks who came to Sanctuary that summer. Although some kids from affluent homes took advantage of Sanctuary's facilities, the great majority of the kids discussed here came from working-class or lower-middle-class families. Seventeen of the individuals originated in metropolitan Boston, with the others coming from as far away as New Orleans and Chicago.

Many kids came to the hostel simply to find a place to stay and perhaps to meet and talk with others. The individuals we discuss form a slightly special case: they spent a relatively large amount of time with staff people and had significant conflicts which they had to work through. Even considering *all* the young people who came to Sanctuary, however, does not give a totally representative picture of street people, because some were able to make it—in terms of emotional as well as physical needs—completely on their own. If this book overplays the problematic side of living on the streets, the tendency reflects the experiences of the individuals with whom Sanctuary had the most extensive, in-depth contact. If all the kids seem to be emotionally tortured or stranded, it is important to remember that the staff often saw them in the midst of their crises. The young people also had to face their problems without the traditional sources of support available to adolescents—family, school, stable peer groups—although Sanctuary tried, as far as it was able, to fill these gaps. The staff found that kids on the streets had, on the whole, as much character strength as any comparable group of happy, high-school students; they differed from their peers in their lack of contentment and their unwillingness, possibly inability, to kowtow to convention.

When the pronoun "we" appears on these pages, it refers to the two authors, Judith Smith and Jeffrey Blum. When we want to ascribe experiences or a point of view to Sanctuary as a group, we will say "the counselors" or "the staff." Most of the time our own views happen to represent those of the organization, but sometimes they do not.

After Judith Smith graduated from Radcliffe, she began to work as a counselor in June 1970 at Sanctuary. In January 1971, she started to write this book and teach in several of Sanctuary's educational projects. She counseled several of the people in this book, had some dealings with others, and knew almost all of them. Her experience counseling at Sanctuary during the summer of 1970 forms the core of this book. Jeff Blum graduated in 1970 from Harvard, where he was an editor of the *Crimson.* In writing this book, he has utilized his past experience as a journalist and as an editor for a New York City agency newsletter. After joining the Sanctuary staff Jeff Blum talked at length with the counselors in preparing in-depth descriptions of the kids and discussions of the cases. He interviewed other individuals, gathered necessary background materials, and prepared the final manuscript. He is currently the Assistant Director for Research at The Sanctuary.

We have tried to disguise the cases so that even a relative of the people described could not recognize the young people with any degree of certainty. Sometimes this has required extensive disguises. We understand that in doing so we risk distorting the meaning of the cases, but we felt that this was necessary to protect the kids' peace of mind, and to prevent publication of the cases from harming them in any manner. In ways this might have been a neater book if we had limited the cases somehow—to underage runaways, for example, or to kids who had had contact with, say, reform schools. We were, however, trying to develop an overall view of the problems and questions which Sanctuary's kids had to face, and such a selective approach did not seem feasible. Instead, we wrote about the cases which posed the greatest challenge for us, and for this reason, were also of the most concern.

To avoid stuffiness, we sometimes call the adolescents and post-adolescents described in this book "kids," hopefully without the condescension which often accompanies that word. Throughout this book we will refer to the third person as "she" rather than the conventional "he." Although this does not mean that everyone in the book is a woman, we have chosen to reverse the customary usage.

Most of the Sanctuary counselors had not completed any degree program certifying them to be counselors, though a few had worked as social workers and family therapists in the past. They all considered themselves nonprofessionals on the job, though they had regular psychiatric consultation available both as a group and as individuals. The dozen regular staff people ranged in age from nineteen to thirty years, with most of them in their mid twenties. In addition to their potential for being effective counselors, they were chosen because they shared in some ways the kids' alienation from many aspects of current American society. It was hoped that they might act not only as friends, but also as badly needed advocates for the kids.

During the summer of 1970 and since then, the staff has tried to make the storefront and hostel into places where authentic relationships can develop. The counselors try to be honest with their own feelings as much as they try to be in touch with the kids' emotions. They believe that trust and genuine relationships can develop only in risking some of one's own personality with another person and in opening up and perhaps becoming a little vulnerable. The Sanctuary's counselors do not want to sit back and help so-called patients clarify their problems or analyze the symptoms of their pathology. The staff wants to be involved with the kids as they work through their crises; the counselors want the kids to participate as much as possible as equals in this process. Counselors work against the tendency to make the young people fit their lives into textbook psychology. This is not to say that the counselors (and the authors) never think anyone is sick, but rather that we have different—perhaps broader—standards of health than the rest of society, and also a different perspective on the origins of the sickness of kids.

This approach, however, is easier to describe than to follow. It sometimes becomes tempting to employ the principle of *not* imposing one's own views and values on the kids simply to evade becoming actively involved with what the kids are experiencing. Even when a counselor wishes to become meaningfully involved, it becomes as difficult as it is necessary to set limits on the relationship: although a counselor might want to be a supportive but critical older friend, kids may sometimes want them to be a parent or a lover. Despite the fact that counselors struggle against setting themselves up as having all the answers, many factors operate against maintaining equality even in the unstructured counseling situation at Sanctuary. The situation of the kids, who often have only the hostel and the counselors to rely on contrasts sharply with that of the counselors, who have homes of their own and usually their own friends and lovers. The counseling relationship also gives the counselors "natural" authority, which complicates the goal of equality. The staff works at having resources, information, and contacts which the kids need; the counselors will remain at Sanctuary after the kids depart; in addition, staff members are somewhat older and already have begun to work through some of the conflicts which the kids are just beginning to face. Counselors must work at neither escaping nor abusing the reality of their own authority, or they run the risk of being classed with other authorities which kids—and often counselors themselves—have learned to dislike and often rebel against. Having relinquished the official air, the processing procedures, and the one-hour-a-week regimen of traditional social work agencies, the counselors are left with only their own resources to use in making contacts and in setting limits on relationships.

Although we believe that people's conflicts are seldom purely personal but often result from the way society is set up, economically as well as bureaucratically, that alone does not tell us how to deal with these problems or what to say to these people. It is a moot point whether or not a young person's troublesome situation is her "fault"; her life is still her own, to do with what she can. Sometimes practical, individual solutions—getting a job, or an apartment, or even returning home—give people the confidence and strength they need to survive. Sometimes a good trusting relationship with a Sanctuary counselor gives a young person the hope she needs to keep on trying to make it in an often impersonal, sometimes hostile, world. Or at least that's what we and the staff need to believe to keep on going; we know that many kids move on entirely untouched by our influence, and that some whom we have failed may be worse off than when they came to us.

In critical ways society has abandoned these "street people" and other dropouts. Case after case showed that these kids have absolutely nowhere to turn: no liveable home, no meaningful work, no relevant schooling, few ways for them to become fully involved either with their peers or the community. Staff members were deeply conflicted about how best to counsel. On the one hand, counselors knew that many of the kids had trouble in the ways they related to other people; and the staff felt that building strong relationships with them would be helpful here. Faced with the kids' lack of resources, however, talking and building personal relationships alone seemed insufficient. Since the kids' problems were larger than personal issues, counselors believed that individual counseling would only be meaningful if it went with attempts to change the society which had abandoned them.

This desertion is manifested by the lack of writing which attempts to evaluate honestly the forces behind the kids' leaving home and what they finally find on the streets or to appraise counseling facilities designed to aid them. Our society's dislocations—broken home, alcoholism, drug addiction, crime, war, and racism—are not likely to simply go away, but are rather increasing in a frightening manner. We are not going to stop at bemoaning the unraveling of the communal fabric; Americans have thought the family was falling apart ever since twenty years after they landed at Plymouth Rock. But today we are faced with vast numbers of kids running away, more kids being incarcerated in "therapeutic" institutions which cannot even tame them, let alone help them. This book is designed to share our experiences. We think, perhaps naively, that a fresh viewpoint *can* help.

Sometimes our discussions might lead the reader to believe that we think that all people are good and that society acts mainly as a giant corrupting influence. We are not sure what we think about the morality or goodness of human beings in their natural state; we have, however, observed the ways society does them serious injustice. We do not consider the Sanctuary staff missionaries who are helping the innocent victims (street people) against the agents of the evil society; rather, we believe that everyone who lives under imperialism (even Americans), under capitalism (even rich people), under sexism (even men), and under racism (even whites) is oppressed. People who have no alternative but the streets are simply more oppressed, although they are not always conscious of it.

Sanctuary counselors for the summer of 1970 included: Noelle Caskey, Tom Faulkner, co-founder of the Sanctuary, Katie Gressle, Richard Gressle, current Associate Director, Stephen Guthrie, Peter Haynes, Tom Howard, Sylvia Hyde, Richard Johnson, Marc Kashnor, Rick Margolin, Susan Scrivenor, Judith Smith, Marianne Spitzform, Craig Thomas, Ray Thomas, Debbie Towne, and Ronald White.

The suggestions and work of many people have gone into this book; it is as much the product of the whole Sanctuary staff as it is that of the two authors. Sanctuary counselor Steven Ward wrote "Summer Travelers," and helped us with other chapters. Other staff members–especially Melinda Liu, Pope Brock, Richard Bock, Martha McCahill and Abigail English, as well as our friends Jeffrey Baker, Larry Blum, and Elizabeth Spelke–also helped greatly in the work. Joan Griffin, Alison Berry, Muriel Gould, and Jeanne Colbeth aided us in the final preparation of the manuscript. Carol Garlington was our editor, and Linda Scovill designed the lay-out and cover of the book. Finally, the book could not have been written without the guidance and encouragement of Sanctuary's director, the Reverend David L. Bynum.

SUMMER TRAVELERS

Throughout the summer of 1970, Sanctuary's storefront and hostel became a way station in the routes of summer travelers headed across the country and as a result, a point of contact between older hippies on the road and teenage street people based in Cambridge. Aside from specific crises—counselors hustling off to the hospital with a kid who had hepatitis, or off to a lawyer with a kid busted on the Common—the storefront was the scene of a continuing interaction between older freaks and Cambridge's runaways.

Two distinct worlds of experience intersected in the storefront. Many of the older longhairs were college students, or one-time college students, who were more worldly and often more at equilibrium than Sanctuary's street people. The summer travelers for the most part were children of the middle class (unlike most street kids who were apt to be runaways from working-class homes) and demonstrated a middle-class ability to take advantage of contacts in unfamiliar cities, to scout out free food, and free entertainment. Being more enterprising, the summer travelers tended to have shorter stays at Sanctuary and were less likely to hang around the storefront, indoors and idle, on sunny afternoons. Perhaps because of time spent in college, the older travelers seemed more likely to be in touch with friends in all corners of the country. Hitch-hiking around the country, they would follow routes connecting a roommate, an old hometown, a one-time commune, an old friend. Sanctuary's hostel provided a temporary stop for people who managed to be quite comfortable in moving from coast to coast in this manner.

In contrast, Cambridge's street population consists of working-class young people, who are often fleeing in-tolerable home situations. Those under eighteen run a real risk of being jailed or being returned to their parents every time they venture out on an interstate highway. It is illegal for children under eighteen to leave home without permission. Because most runaways can't conceal their age, their sense of vulnerability prompts the kind of angry defensiveness which can turn a ticket for highway speeding into a dope bust or a runaway arrest. As a result Cambridge's summer street population includes a great many penniless teenagers who don't manage to get even as far from the Common as the White Mountains, or the North Shore beaches. Ironically, kids are drawn from stalemated home situations by a myth of easy gratification in Cambridge only to discover that what little security they find there vanishes as soon as they are out of sight of the Prudential Tower. The myth draws desperate kids to Cambridge and the likelihood of police harassment often prohibits their leaving, except out of further desperation.

Another factor, however, also contributes to the phenomenon of kids wandering around with their back-packs and sleeping bags in the city, rather than in the country where they might learn to live in a more self-sufficient manner. Street kids often said they were in Cambridge for only a few days: that they had just come in from Berkeley, for example, and they were soon heading on to Montreal. From the atmosphere within the Sanctuary hostel, however, it appeared that kids were not going to the country partially because they were simply afraid to move out there alone. The kids were lonely, and that seemed to be a major reason they stayed in the city where the people were; most of them were not ready for the solitude of the wide open spaces—not yet.

The Cambridge Common is the focus of all the restlessness that arriving runaways bring with them. Like Telegraph Avenue in Berkeley, or the Old Quarter in New Orleans, the Common promises anonymity, plentiful drugs (buying grass, speed, or acid offers people a chance to make a connection to find a place to stay), and a turf that is recognized as a reservation for street hippies, criminals, and outsiders—teenagers all. Life on the Common is a fluid sequence of conversational contacts, regular rip-offs, and a constant parade of sexual posturings that recall the elaborate hair-combing rituals of motorcycle-jacketed teenagers of another era. Finally, life on the Common is an experience of tedium, movement in aimless revolutions around the memorial pedestal, from which Lincoln surveys the new emancipation. The tedium is punctuated only by the great clouds of dust which Charles River breezes sweep across the Common (little grass has survived for four years now), and by intermittent police surveys, in which newcomers and small-time heroin sellers alike are pushed away from the slogan-covered Common gates and indiscriminately busted.

Street kids bring this dispirited sense of being trapped in an aimless and endless cycle with them to Sanctuary and to their encounters with older, traveling hippies. These encounters emphasize the language which both groups have in common and the music which both share. The older travelers use drugs less frequently, and in a clearly less self-destructive way; in some respects they suggest older brothers and sisters to the younger, more disillusioned breed of youngsters. In the summer of 1970 the older travelers represented two groups: college kids who had come unglued from the values and expectations of college career training in the aftermath of Kent State, and seasoned hippies who, en route from scene to scene in couples, sometimes married, had been living a free-form life for years. Both college and hippie travelers were quite capable of feeling at home in their temporary environment at Sanctuary. They enjoyed focusing restless energies in impromptu music-making or getting engaged in raps about travel adventures, trip adventures, spiritual adventures.

These travelers represented an ideal of self-sufficiency and free-spirited optimism which for street people was made unreachable by the grinding realities of street life. During one morning shift in the storefront last summer, a knot of street kids gathered at the mouth of the narrow back door hallway, apparently attracted by something visible in the backyard.

The storefront is a single room, forty feet by thirty feet, with big windows fronting the street. It is split into two areas: one with raised, carpeted platforms as a space for relaxing, rapping, which became kind of a street people's living room; the other a desk area for three phones, three semicubicles for quiet talking, a counter for free food and coffee, and a private staff and counseling office. The cellar is used for storing baggage; there is also a bathroon and wash-up area, separated from the staff office by a narrow hallway.

In the backyard a guy named Tom, a ponytailed Californian on the road for the summer, and his wife, Marie, were going individually through yoga exercises. They had stayed at the hostel the night before, relaxed at the storefront after washing up and were starting the day, apparently like any other, with yoga. Most of the kids bunched at the back door had no acquaintance with yoga;

they thought what Tom and Marie were doing looked odd—like slow-motion calisthentics—but they seemed impressed by the couple's deliberateness. When a counselor told Mark, one of the street kids, that what they were watching was yoga, he smiled and said he had never seen it before. The counselor suggested that anybody probably could join Tom and Marie and ask them about it, but the group at the back hallway was quick to drift away from the door.

When the married couple reentered the storefront, however, and began organizing their baggage, Mark approached Tom, and, without pretending to be knowledgeable about yoga, asked him how long he had been doing those exercises. A relaxed conversation followed in which two other street kids joined, listening quietly. Somehow, this whole incident suggests many of the imponderables underlying the encounters between street kids and long term hippies in the storefront. Looking down the hallway into the back yard, Mark was unwilling to take the steps to learn something about yoga, although he was curious enough about it to approach Tom later in a more impersonal situation inside the storefront. The conversation that followed seemed to be one in which each was open to the other; it assumed a common trust from its beginning. Mark's voice contained a kind of envy that Tom evidently had learned to use a discipline that he drew strength from. Despite their mutual use of hip jargon, the real contrast between them was in the way that each spoke: Mark, eager with questions, quick—sometimes extravagant—in his reactions; Tom slower, more impassive, his speech deliberate, composed. It seemed that Mark was attentive to this difference and was wondering how to account for it.

Intermittently throughout the summer, conversations of this sort occurred in loose gatherings of twos, threes, fours on Sanctuary's platforms. The long-haired travelers brought to the storefront stories of busts, highs, and deliverance from abysmal situations; what the Sanctuary street kids took from these conversations were impressions of a meaningful way of living outside of the umbrella of nine-to-five, work-a-day, "life insurance" America. For Cambridge's insular street population, between the lines of these impromptu conversations, was confidence that there was a rich world of experience to be shared, outside of the Common's dusty cycles of rap and rip-off, and, more important, that the older brothers and sisters who moved in that world seemed to have found a sense of purpose there.

How rare on the Common–a sense that living has credible purposes. Street people speak of survival as an accomplishment, and rightly so in Cambridge. To the summer travelers, though, survival might well seem only the barest of minimums. Street people then sought out on Sanctuary's platforms that confidence in the healthiness of the hippie myth which the travelers brought with them. Or perhaps it was the street kids who endowed the travelers with that confidence, needing to find signs of faith in what *Newsweek* calls the counterculture.

Some travelers, like Tom, brought that faith with them; in the form of morning yoga it was made explicit and perceptible. For others, it was communicated in a confident rapping about past trials, in energetic guitar-playing, or in that kind of amusement at one's own expense in which personal ups and downs are placed in the context of melodrama. Street people, for their part, began to talk more about the ideal of viewing the scene on the Common and in Sanctuary as one composed of brothers and sisters in the same boat, rather than competitors for spare change or plotters of rip-off schemes. Kids in the storefront, for example, would speak of their sisters on the street, hesitantly to be sure, as if female runaways deserved more than just the protection of the men, who were, not infrequently, pimps to whom they were attached. The uncertainties about whether to regard girls on the street as sisters, or short-haired AWOLs as brothers came naturally. When the street is a community, it is one without a developed economy; in this system sex is as much a commodity of survival as spare change. And in the absence of other ways for female runaways to get by, male street people are often entirely willing to take advantage of their dependence.

Sex roles and the status of females on the streets are not radically dissimilar from the traditional patterns of the larger society. These young women did not always seem to be in control of their sexual situations. Just as they would have trouble telling their parents about their encounters, so they had considerable hesitancy about confiding in women counselors, even when they seemed to want to discuss sex. Men were no better and, in some ways, worse than their peers in "straight" society. Many boys considered their girl, and all girls in general, as objects, even though sometimes coveted possessions.

From the counselors' viewpoint, the Cambridge street scene bore out the idea that some effects of the "sexual revolution" are even more oppressive to women than the *ancien regime's* regimen of monogamy. Repeatedly, these young women were led into sexual relations they did not want because to have refused to sleep with a man would have been "unfair" to him and would have meant that they were as outdated as brassieres. Admittedly, females who were known to have slept with several men were not ostracized as they might have been in their high school communities. But the opposite ethic of the streets is not better: for an adolescent to feel committed to sleeping with everyone is as oppressive as to feel that one must not sleep with anyone. Even in rural communes, sex roles are preserved: the males chop the wood, and the females bake the bread. The situation described here is not a result of the street culture, but a carryover of the sex roles and attitudes from the kids' original communities.

Randy, a seventeen-year-old runaway from Florida, got into a fight on the Common for telling a Roxbury teenager, male and probably a pimp, to quit hassling a blond runaway girl called Sunshine. Sunshine was able to split the Common as the fight got broken up. But this kind of intervention on behalf of brothers and sisters, going beyond lip service, is dangerous, confusing, and often pointless. Not infrequently, street women are insulted that a male expects to protect *their* interest, sometimes out of a Sisterhood Is Powerful consciousness, sometimes out of an opposite feeling, anger that someone should mess up a game when the payoff–a place to stay for a night or two, a protector and confidante on the street–is within sight. Moreover, the fact that many of these protectors are black submerges the whole issue in the larger and more dangerous conflicts of racial coexistence on the street.

The Common is a composite of shifting sets of expectations–about survival, sex, hippie ideology, race–and street people bring these confusions with them to Sanctuary, and to their contacts with the hippie travelers they meet there. It's easy for street people to get caught between these conflicting nets of expectations. While wishing to identify with the hippie myth, with the blend of self-sufficiency and compassion, street people can get trapped in the contradictions between that ideal and the survival games of the street.

Tripper

A big, red-haired kid called Tripper drifted into the storefront in June; the events of his summer document the development of these confusions. He came to Harvard Square to be a hippie or summer traveler but he was defeated by the needs of survival on the streets. His deterioration was made all the more painful for Sanctuary because we were helpless to affect its causes. Tripper was nineteen, and therefore legal, having hitchhiked to Cambridge from a poor milltown in Pennsylvania. He moved through the flow of street people on the Common and in Harvard Square with a consistent good humor and a kind of grace that may have come from his seniority (relative to runaways) and his belief in himself and in hippieness.

During his first week in Cambridge he came to Sanctuary tripping on acid. His trip was an exuberant one. He lay on his back on the platform and yelled to street people and staff members: "You're beautiful, this place is beautiful." Then a big grin, and he would add, "Cambridge is beautiful too." Tripper's sunny nature was partially supported by his skill at leatherwork; he would spontaneously make a gift of a belt to a newly met "brother freak," as he put it. Later he may well have regretted such naive generosity.

In the storefront he once talked about his family, but with a kind of disturbingly cheerful detachment, recalling laughingly his constant fighting with his father. Tripper seemed glad to be in Cambridge, enjoying the street scene he found there without identifying with it. A shift began to occur as the summer wore on, and police pressures increased. The staff Log Book, a daily diary of impressions of the storefront, documents it.

> July 1: Tripper is in here. He's crashing from speed, has the shakes, is incredibly down. He's really been hit with the fact that he has to find a job and a place.

> July 7: Tripper got a job doing something with leather through city employment. I woke him up this morning at the hostel in time to get there, and we looked at the map to see where it was he was

going. I met him later that day on the street. He looked a little down, said the job was some complicated process he didn't know how to do.

August 3: Tripper came in to the hostel around 2 a.m. He said he'd been kicked out of the place where he was staying. He said he didn't do stuff around the house, like take out the garbage, and the other people got mad. He looked pretty shook up, said he couldn't talk much, said his lip was bleeding. I think he'd been in a fight.

August 9: Tripper seems really incoherent, and almost hostile. He's farther out than ever, speaks constantly in word games and patterns. Ever since he took acid with Purple Haze, another street kid, he's been acting strange: he said that he'd been on Haze's trip involved with the devil and Jehovah. He decided to go see the shrink at the free clinic this afternoon.

August 15: A kid ran into the storefront and said that Tripper has been arrested, that he fought the police, and that he's in the city hospital. The report turns out to be true. As the police were busting kids for dope on the Common, Tripper was arrested for loitering and somehow ended up in the hospital with a broken rib and 12 stitches. Several other people were arrested along with him.

August 20: Tripper spent the night before his trial in jail because we couldn't get him bail. He looked confused and weak in court, but otherwise okay. At the insistence of the court physician he is being put into a mental health center. His case has been continued for three months while Tripper is in the hospital for observation.

Tripper's story is a speeded-up movie of a process that is continually occurring on the street. People arrive at Harvard Square eager to "see what's happening," to compare distant impressions of the hip life in Cambridge with what's visible on the Common; finding very little that corresponds to their expectations, they get lost in the shuffle of drugs, people, and values and end up identifying with the aimlessness and waste of the street. Tripper's exit from the street isn't unusual; other people leave for home or prison instead of mental hospitals. Only occasionally do people wake up to the circles they're caught in and decisively make a break for a rural commune or a fulltime job in the city, or return to free-form movement on the road.

We stayed in touch with Tripper for the month he was in the mental health center; he seemed isolated and depressed to the point that he was murmuring more than talking. As a result of his trial, Tripper was admitted to a mental hospital in Pennsylvania and then released to his parents. He's home now, although we've received no word from him.

Tripper threw away one asset that set him apart initially from street people: he could have travelled legally and freely around the country. In the course of the summer he lost sight of the freedom that brought him to Cambridge in the first place. Simply put, Tripper came to Cambridge to be a hippie. Perhaps he was naive in imagining that he only needed to arrive in Cambridge and a hippie life style would be assured for him. Certainly he became confused by the discovery that amidst the Common's hustle, being a hippie may mean being a fool. A gesture of generosity, like the gift of the handmade belt, could be mistaken as an opportunity for rip-off.

Despite Tripper's expectations of Cambridge as a hippie scene, there are in fact scant supports, moral or economic, for hippie subsistence in Cambridge. Tripper didn't expect to have to do leatherwork all summer, so he was relieved, in part, when his tools were stolen in mid-summer. He had a harder and harder time getting spare change to live on in the street: in June, Tripper's charm made him a dazzling spare-change artist, but by July his spare-changing was bringing in less the more desperate he felt about it.

Tripper was in some sense the victim of the same hippie myth which he had broadcast with such verve upon his arrival in Cambridge. That myth, although admirably suited to the needs of the older travelers who appeared in Sanctuary's storefront, is continually at odds with the survival requirements of life on the Common; Tripper, for one, became increasingly confused–to the point of immobilization–as the contradictions became unbearable.

RUNAWAYS

Adolescent development is a complex process in any age. Today it is made especially difficult by recent trends and events: open sexuality, the widespread use of illegal drugs such as marihuana, the increasing availability of stronger drugs, and the divisive conflicts about the war in Southeast Asia. After college students, both black and white, were killed in protests against the invasion of Cambodia in May 1970, kids began to question the traditional assumptions about free speech in America. When a Black Panther leader was bound and gagged throughout the long Chicago Conspiracy Trial, kids noted the sharp discrepancy between the way their textbooks described courtroom justice and what actually happened. These kinds of pressures must be considered in addition to the particular pressures of individual families as part of the configuration causing kids to run away from home. No one-to-one correlation exists between society's problems and any one child running away from her home, but we cannot discuss the failings of families without talking about the society which in part defines how each member of the family perceives herself in relation to the others.

With divorce, alcoholism, and crime rates climbing each year, it appears to be the society itself that is profoundly unstable—not just some especially unfortunate families. Kids are not the only ones who feel the disturbing pressures of the time; parents, too, are victims of forces beyond their control. Grownups do not become alcoholics or desert their spouses out of either spite or a desire to hurt their offspring. Men are dissatisfied with their jobs and women are locked up in linoleum kitchens, both caught up in dreams of material goods and sexual partners which in fact have not brought happiness, or even the strength to continue with good grace. One cannot ultimately distinguish between the quality of interaction in the institutions of society and the quality of interaction of individuals in the home, which is, after all, society's paradigmatic institution. Families train their children to succeed at adapting to the larger society; this is usually called socialization. Living within the context of parental authority instructs young people to accept the authority, or power, of other hierarchical institutions: governments, business firms, and universities.

Yet this process can also work in another way: although society and specific families do not affect each other in direct, causal ways, widespread and viscerally felt changes in the ways individuals perceive society can affect how they perceive the structures of their own families. It seems easier to detect this effect in times of rapid change, like today. As young people see authority undermined and questioned on every front, in their own homes as well as through the media, it is natural that they will feel the authority which affects them most, that of the family, to grow more palpable, perhaps oppressive, and possibly intolerable. It also becomes more natural and therefore possible, to test the family's authority, just as across the country individuals are testing all kinds of authority. For example, about half the young people in this country perceive the war in Vietnam as immoral. They therefore either plan to refuse induction into the armed services or start plotting to get a deferment. In addition to refusing to serve in the war, many young men and women feel that they should not cooperate with or obey the authority that conducts the war–a feeling that spreads to every kind of authority which seems to support that government, including the family.

Poor kids–and black kids–realize that no matter how good they are or how hard they work at jobs which society often considers menial, they will not graduate to acceptance and a house in the suburbs. Accordingly, they reject not only the society that creates those conditions, but also sometimes those parents who more or less consciously instill the society's values. Some kids become disenchanted with the effect competition has on personal interactions, and also with the failure of the fruits of that competition, success, to provide meaning or contentment. They loudly question the fathers and mothers whose jobs force them to compete and who seem to make success and its correlate, popularity, the paramount value for young people.

In New York City and Chicago the number of warrants issued for runaway children *has doubled* in the past seven years, and the number of runaways is increasing even more rapidly in the suburbs; sensible estimates put the total number of runaways at around a million (*Newsweek*, October 26, 1970, p. 67). This phenomenon reflects primarily society-wide, not just personal, changes and problems. Possibly individual families just are not built the way they used to be; this may be true in some ways. However, one needs to ask why families seem to be falling apart, how the objective conditions have changed so as to make it harder for families to survive together, harder for men, women, and children to accept the limits of family roles. It is inaccurate to consider the often broken homes of runaways as if they existed in a vacuum. When working with runaways, a counselor not only must consider the personal problems, but also must be conscious of the relevant social issues, conflicts, and failings. Struggling with society's latent, unresolved conflicts may be a real and immediate dilemma for adolescents.

HOME AND THE STREETS

The immense difficulties of growing up in America today lead many young people to seek out the attractions and adventures of the streets. The current rate of technological change makes inherited morality inadequate; adults as well as kids are on their own. Growing up, as always, depends on experience in the world outside the family and the chance to assimilate challenges. Kids need to be able to test the larger community and to find out that they can survive in it on their own. The contradictions and chaos within our culture make living a confusing and baffling proposition for everyone and thus make adolescents' needs for experience and competence that much more intense.

Kids need a place in the community to venture forth from with freedom and also to retreat to for support with no questions asked. Adolescents feel the need to be able to travel, to have jobs, to experiment with living arrangements, and to maintain a secure home base. Learning and growth are not restricted to classrooms; development can take place anywhere as long as kids sense themselves to be independent people in real situations. Kids need energy and faith in themselves to be able to overcome the isolation of adolescence by risking a little of themselves in the wider, adult community.

Right now in American society, it feels as if the cornerstones of kids' lives, family and school, stand in the way of their freedom to make their own mistakes, to seize their own opportunities, and to define themselves in a manner that seems fitting with their growth. Parents say they want their kids to be mature and independent, but in fact they limit their children's access to the world and heap disapproval on the few attempts they make to decide things for themselves and to live independently. The community passes laws to keep kids in school and at home, frowns on long hair and other expressions of youth and sensuality, and self-righteously covers itself with American flags to contrast adults' patriotism with kids' antiwar protest. Schools repress kids' tremendous energies, isolate them from the life of their community, and often refuse to make use of or even recognize kids' own experiences. Kids commonly graduate from school, if they stick it out that long, with feelings of deadness and little self-confidence.

The pressures at home and school are different for young men than for young women, and consequently they look for slightly different things on the streets. Little is well articulated, but it seems that the boys are more pressured about success, doing well in school and getting jobs, while the girls are more confined by rules governing social behavior. Both dislike what they see in their parent's lives: men and women tied down to unfulfilling and often dehumanizing jobs, either in a factory or in an office, and women further constrained by stifling housework and child care. Many kids are conscious and accepting of their inability to fit into standard, high school sex roles. Girls cannot and do not aspire to be cute, flirty dates who take typing courses, and boys feel the same about being big stud football players who understand cars. They refuse to compete at conforming, to be successful in someone else's terms.

Young people perceive the streets as offering what is denied by family and school: first-hand confrontation with the world and a chance to experience what it is like to survive on your own—in short, a competence test that *counts.* What could be more real? The streets promise the very adventure and risk that is otherwise missing and hold out the prospect of sharing its dangers with one's contemporaries and forming deep relationships in the process. Some kids on the street seem beautiful and innocent and also worldly beyond their years as they sit at Sanctuary and recount their travels. A few kids flourish: their independence seems to help them live freely and become more mature. Other kids, however, are markedly less fortunate. Their lives on the streets are at least as emotionally barren as the atmospheres of the homes they left behind, if not more so; they seem alone and lost.

The media present the cities of San Francisco, Berkeley, Cambridge, Portland, and Madison as living communities where people accept and care about each other. Street culture seems to hold out new worlds, including liberated sex and bountiful drugs. According to the myth, the most socially inept high school girl from Kalamazoo and the most uncoordinated would-be basketball player from Kansas City need only throw beads around their necks, tie-dye their undershirts, grab sleeping bags and turn to the streets to find excitement and fulfillment. Being misunderstood and mistreated at home, miserable and ignored at school doesn't matter; you can leave it all for a community of your equals, your friends. No parents allowed, just kids. Knowledge is not contained in books but in hallucinogens; and it is certainly easier to swallow acid than to read books. No rules—no limits. The world seems to belong to those who go out on the streets and seize it.

All young people feel these pressures and contradictions to varying degrees. Each responds to them in her own way, although some do not react to them in any more discernible manner than to wear their hair a trifle longer.

Some turn dissatisfactions inward and respond to their feelings of inadequacy in a personal way; some withdraw, others steal hubcaps. Considering the scope of the phenomenon, running away seems to parallel the other youth movements that are underway in the nation. Many kids known as "weekend hippies" technically live at home but spend every spare moment on the streets. Other kids, especially those, say, under twenty, are rejecting the importance of attending school and are working instead of going to college. Kids who see their personal conflicts as reflections of social issues are joining together to change things. Sit-ins, walk-outs, and strikes, already common in colleges, are rapidly becoming so on the secondary school level. Running away seems to be an extreme rather than an atypical mode of response.

For all this, it is still often impossible to explain why one kid leaves home and another, with pressures that seem similar, remains. But then it is always more difficult to fathom why people behave "normally," in the sense of being like everyone else, than to explain why any one person behaves differently. Family conflicts, many of which are examined throughout this book, have, of course, always existed. But how the conflicts and social pressures are interacting today to make kids feel trapped so much more intensely–this is what we wish to explore.

NOTES ON COUNSELING RUNAWAYS

It seems important to try to delineate some of the issues which arise in counseling runaways. The first priority is to make contact with the kid: to tell her who you are; to find who she is; to find out why she came to you. It is important not to push kids too much too soon. Give them time to get comfortable with you, to watch you and decide that you can be trusted, that you will neither judge nor threaten them. In practice, this means not demanding that a kid talk about loaded family issues until she is ready to do so and leaving most of the initiative after a first friendly encounter up to her. Sometimes legal emergencies force the process to happen much faster—when the police are on their way to pick up an illegal runaway, for example, it is not fair for anyone to mince words.

From the time the counselor meets a runaway, she should try to figure out why the kid left home. The counselor should ask herself why this particular kid has run away, what she might be trying to say to her parents and to the world. It's important to keep in mind the problems a fourteen-year-old often has in articulating complex issues. She is usually unaccustomed to being verbally explicit about her feelings. The counselor must use all the available clues—what the kid says, what she omits, how she interacts with the other kids around, and how she approaches the staff—to get an idea of what's happening.

Anyone who works with people is familiar with the problem of separating fact from fiction in what an upset stranger tells you. It is important to be aware of this problem, but not to worry about it too much. Instead, think more about whatever fantasies are presented and where they may be coming from; use the fantasies as guides to understanding the kid.

Of course, kids are not the only people who have fantasies. Counselors must be in touch with their own fantasies about running away and with the tendency to project their own needs onto the kids. Since most Americans live in nuclear families—that is, married couples live with their children, while grandparents, aunts, uncles, and so forth maintain separate residences—almost everyone leaves home at one time or another to start a new life. Certainly people who seriously regard themselves as part of a counter culture are specifically defining themselves apart from their parents. All of us at Sanctuary have made breaks with our homes, some sharp, others not so sharp. Accordingly, staff members must watch their tendency to want runaways and other street kids to be able to break away from their families completely and successfully.

It would, therefore, be an error to take kids' desires to run away *too* seriously and to disregard their needs to work through the same basic family conflicts over which we all agonize. We at Sanctuary, like our contemporaries across the country, have some doubts that the nuclear family system is necessarily the best way to bring up children. But no matter what we think of nuclear families, it is undeniable that we all grew up in them and that they produce certain conflicts which must be worked out though not necessarily at home, before an adolescent can either become successfully independent of her family or start new, mature patterns of relationships as an adult. If an adolescent cannot resolve serious childhood conflicts, these same questions will probably recur through her life cycle; although it is a moot point whether or not daughters bear the sins of their mothers, it seems evident that they must struggle with the weight of their parents' conflicts.

As has been stated before, very few satisfactory alternatives exist for kids who feel that they must leave home. Until other stable and warm arrangements for kids are developed, the family continues to be the only place equipped with the resources and sense of responsibility necessary for kids to live. There are two speculative "ifs": if we lived in extended family groups so that a kid could move in with a cousin until things cooled off or where her aunt could manage to adopt her if her father spent all his money on alcohol, or if the counterculture were more cohesive, and childless couples were more interested in the fate of kids, then maybe things would be different.

In dealing with runaways, the kids are actually only half the situation; family counseling or therapy seems to be necessary if reintegration into the family is the desired goal. But since Sanctuary's most important job is making contact with kids, when they ask us not to call their parents, staff members don't, because it might endanger the rapport the counselors are trying to establish with the kids. The staff believes that Sanctuary's uniqueness as a service and whatever possibilities for genuinely reaching kids it possesses come from its ability to form trusting relationships with kids. When any runaway comes in, an immediate alternative offered is work with the family. But when kids refuse that offer, as many of them do, the staff feels that they must respect that choice. The staff believes that when kids are ready to talk with their families, they'll come back and ask us to arrange it. Some kids do just that.

Many parents call up or come in to report that their children are missing and to ask Sanctuary's help in locating them. All the counselors can do, however, when they recognize a kid, is to inform her that her parents are actively looking for her and that they care about what happens to her. With the parents, however, the staff is in a good position to try to get them to focus on why their kids left, as well as to discuss life on the streets and why kids need to try it out.

The counselor can often help the runaway by acting as a reality check. By trying to verify whether or not the situation is really as bad or as impossible as the kid perceives it to be, she can help straighten out the kid's confusions. Kids involved in youth culture identities often have some values which are markedly different from those of their parents; a counselor can clarify the difference and point out the shared ideas. The counselor is also in a good position to help balance the power in a family confrontation by helping the kid articulate what's on her mind. At the same time they try to chart the kids' confusions and problems, the counselors want very much to be in touch with the healthy and positive sides of the kids they deal with. It is crucial to take seriously the complaints and dilemmas which kids present rather than treating them as the result of a bundle of Freudian complexes.

RUNNING AWAY TO SPEAK TO PARENTS

In most of Sanctuary's runaway cases, the kids refer to a specific incident or case of mistreatment which, they say, "caused" their running away. It is our experience that these specific incidents–getting punished for smoking dope or for failing at school, and so forth–are usually real and sometimes too difficult for the kids to handle alone. That the families could not manage the situation in a way that would make the household livable for the child is symptomatic of deeper and more pervasive conflicts.

Fran and Susie

Some kids run away to say something very important, very immediate, and very powerful to their parents. Fran and Susie did this. They came into the storefront together, toward the end of August. They looked young, unsure of themselves, and scared. Randy, the counselor on duty, invited them into the office to talk. They opened up immediately, saying they were runaways from Manchester, New Hampshire, and were headed for the west coast with six dollars between the two of them.

Fran, a tall, unusual-looking red-headed girl with green eyes and pale skin, started talking first. She very quickly swung the conversation to her home situation, about which she was anxious and ready to talk. She was sixteen and had five older brothers and sisters, each of whom had left home at about her age without finishing high school. Fran's parents were always pushing her to be better than the others, to finish high school and go on to college. Fran, thrusting her chin forward, said that she didn't think *she* wanted to finish school either. She was pretty sure she could get a job as a model and wasn't about to put up with the drudgery of her high school any longer than legally necessary. Fran didn't have enough freedom at home; she had to be in too early, and her parents asked too many questions. Her father drank too much, she said, and was mean when he was drunk. She was afraid of him; he had once threatened to break both of her legs. He had suffered a heart attack the previous year, and whenever Fran threatened opposition to her parents' wishes, they responded by saying she would kill her father with her tantrums.

Susie, a small fifteen-year-old girl with short, curly, blonde hair which she kept hidden by a scarf, was neither as strong nor as articulate as Fran. She wasn't able to look directly at Randy when the three of them were talking together; instead she often glanced at Fran for support. All she would say was that she, too, didn't have enough freedom at home. She said that her mother was divorced from her father and that she and her little brother lived with her mother, but she didn't respond to Randy's questions as to how she felt about the situation.

Randy suspected that the young women were unclear about their ideas, so he asked them about their plans for getting to the west coast. They answered that they planned to stay with Fran's older sister, who lived in San Francisco. At Randy's suggestion, they called her, and from his end of the conversation, it sounded as if the sister was not overjoyed to hear from the girls. She didn't offer to help them get out there, which they had been half hoping for, but she did say that they could stay with her if they made it across the country.

Randy continued to talk to the girls about their alternatives. He encouraged them to ask questions about life on the road and tried to answer them honestly. Finally he sat back and asked them directly if what they really wanted was family counseling sessions. The relief on their faces showed that he had discerned their real fears about the trip they outlined and their real desires.

The counselor then called both sets of parents, assured them their daughters were safe, and invited them to come to Sanctuary for a family counseling session the next morning. They agreed to come and also gave permission for the girls to stay overnight in the hostel.

The mothers arrived together the next morning. Fran's father hadn't come because of his heart condition, according to her mother. Susie's session was first. Just before it began, Susie looked at her nervous and fidgeting mother and began to cry. Randy remembered that Susie's initial complaint was lack of freedom and wondered if something else might be going on. With little urging, Susie explained to Randy, through her tears, that her mother had a boyfriend who came to stay at their home on the weekends; her mother packed Susie and her brother off to friends' houses or to a great aunt's house in the next town. Then Susie turned to her mother and said she hated going away for the weekends; she felt like an outsider in her own home and wondered if her mother really loved her or wanted her around at all.

Susie said that she didn't understand her mother's relationship with her boyfriend; why, if he loved her, didn't he want to marry her? She speculated that maybe he didn't want to marry her because of Susie and her brother. Susie's mother then burst into tears herself and grabbed her daughter and hugged her. The two talked for over an hour while Randy said very little. He later said that he was proud of Susie for being able to tell her mother how hurt she was. He was equally proud of Susie's mother for being able to respond to her fifteen-year-old daughter as an adult, talking to her about her relationship with her boyfriend and about the way they all felt in their home.

Fran's session was not so monumental, although she was able to express a lot of her anger about the pressures she felt her parents were unfairly placing on her. Randy intervened more in this session, helping Fran to explain what she meant when she said her father's sickness was used against her and also aiding Fran's mother to understand her almost grown-up daughter's need to make her own decision about continuing school.

Randy helped both families get in touch with a local family counseling agency so that they could continue the work started at Sanctuary. He has heard from both girls, who both consider their running away the event which precipitated their families' talking about the problems they were having in living together.

Fran's and Susie's experience were in many ways simple and satisfying to all parties. As a counselor Randy was able to make contact with the girls as well as to intervene effectively with their families. The continuing family therapy will have an effect far beyond the morning session in Cambridge. Fran and Susie were both eventually able to articulate their problems and concerns to their parents in a way that opened up their parents' capacity to respond. By agreeing to family therapy, the parents were also tangibly trying to make things better. By running away, if only for a night, Fran and Susie forced their parents into a position where they agreed to listen to their daughters.

Billy

Most cases, however, are neither so simple nor so satisfying. When Billy, a sixteen-year-old boy from a small town in

New Jersey, came to Sanctuary early one morning, he refused to call home and didn't want Sanctuary to have anything to do with his parents. He intended to force himself to stay away from home for at least six months, although he said he did plan to return eventually.

Small and slight, Billy had a very soft face and long, brown curls. He was shy and apologetic about asking for help, but it was clear that he was lonely and in some ways relieved to have someone to talk to. Billy said that he was sixteen, had finished his sophomore year in high school, and had left home about a month before. When Erica, the counselor he met when he walked in, asked him about his family, he asked hesitatingly if she really wanted to hear about all that and then began to describe them. He was an only child. His parents were divorced; his mother was married to a teacher in a small town in New Jersey, and his father was an insurance salesman, in Philadelphia. Billy had been shunted back and forth since he was eight years old, spending summers with his father and living the rest of the time with his mother. He basically felt misunderstood and uncared for everywhere.

Two crises had provoked his leaving, he thought. One was his parents' most recent plan to send him to a rigid Catholic boys' boarding school. They said that they were looking out for his future and that the school would get him into a good college, but he felt that they were just trying to get rid of him by sending him away. He had toyed with the idea of going to prep school, just because it would be a way to leave home, but soon after that he came to feel that he would find such an authoritarian institution intolerable.

The other "cause" was more personal and harder to explain. Billy used to sneak out of his house to hang around with some older kids, who eventually became very important to him. As Erica understood it, they were a group of acid freaks who lived on a farm not far from Billy's home town. They talked to Billy about Eastern mysticism and their own communal marriage, and Erica felt that Billy was deeply moved by them. They were probably the most interesting people he had met in a long time; and he perceived their gentleness and lovingness as a sharp and welcome contrast to his parents. He went to their farm and stayed overnight there. Erica didn't think that Billy took drugs with them or was interested in doing so; his mind was just blown by their conceptions of the cosmos and personal relationships, and he was sincerely interested in being with them.

He had gone home and told his parents about his night on the farm and about how moved he was by the commune's warmth toward him and by their faith in Eastern religion. His parents didn't become angry, but rather humiliated him by mocking what he said and felt. So Billy split, and came to Boston.

Erica asked Billy how he felt after having been on his own for a month. He looked up at her and said that he was tired of being by himself, and that he missed people and wanted to find a warm and loving commune to settle down in. Erica asked if he wanted her to call home to get permission for him to stay overnight at the hostel. In a way, he looked tired of being a runaway, as if he would be relieved to find some safe place where he could belong, if only for a few days, like Sanctuary. But, after considering a minute, he refused. He had written to his parents to tell them he was safe and that he was planning to go home for a visit in the spring. They would have to take him seriously if he'd been away that long, he said. Only a long time away from home, he felt, would give him the strength and independence he needed to be his own person in his family. So Billy moved on.

Billy was working out something with his parents which was probably less easy to understand or accept than what Fran and Susie were doing, although he similarly needed support, and his complaints were as valid as those the girls expressed. With some justification, the boy interpreted the whole boarding-school plan as merely another of his parents' attempts to get him off their hands. Although deeply hurt by this facet of the plan, he would have gone to the school except that he knew he would have to conform to the school's rules and expectations. Personal and social factors interacted to cause Billy to run away. He needed to establish himself as an independent person: his parents could neither toss him around like a football nor determine his life style for him. Sanctuary's role in this case was limited to providing a sympathetic and, at the same time, practical person with whom Billy could test his ideas and from whom he could count on a sincere response.

John

Fourteen-year-old John Sullivan, a short and stocky boy who wore jeans and acted tough, came to Sanctuary late in July after spending the previous few nights sleeping down by the river. Dishevelled and tired, John seemed frightened as he wandered tentatively into the hostel. Rich, the counselor on duty, had been watching for him. Earlier the social worker who dealt with John's father had called him to say that, if John came by, he had his father's permission to stay for a few nights. Rich approached John and told him that the social worker had called.

Noticing how uncomfortable the boy looked, he asked him if he'd like to come sit with him on the steps and check people in for the night. Instead of trying immediately to get him to talk about why he had run away, Rich tried to make John feel relaxed and unpressured in the hostel. When his shift ended, he made sure that John had gotten to meet an older, stable guy who knew his way around the place. He also introduced John to the counselor coming in for the overnight, and briefly explained the situation to her.

In the next couple of days, the staff gradually pieced together a picture of what was going on in John's life. John had left his home in a Somerville housing project after his father had hit him in front of a friend for staying out too late. John had felt humiliated and furious. He said his father was generally tense and nervous, and took it out on him. He did well in school, and was beginning to have a crowd of boys and girls his own age to hang around with, but his father disapproved of them, according to John, because they were not "fancy"enough. The boy also felt pressured by his father's high standards; "I won't be his little dream kid," John said fiercely. In an off-hand, too-wise-for-his-years voice, John informed us that his father had had several unhappy affairs recently. None of the women he had been involved with were willing to marry him if they would have to take care of John.

One afternoon when Rich was on duty again, Alice Johnson, the social worker who had called earlier, stopped by. Alice seemed pleasant and informal. She corroborated John's story and told Rich more about John's father whom she considered "too crazy" to take care of his son. Mr. Sullivan had been married and divorced four times. John had been born a few months before his parents were divorced and his mother had deserted his father, making no claim for custody of John. Alice described Mr. Sullivan as attractive, very anxious, and, at the same time, very proud. The man disliked what he called the seediness of his neighborhood, and was furious at its filth. Mr. Sullivan was supported by veteran's disability and he hated that dependent state of existence. To complicate matters, his tension produced frequent asthma attacks, which he tried to control with a constant dosage of tranquilizers. Alice admitted that she had been relieved when Mr. Sullivan had declared that, since John had run away, he didn't want him back in the house. Alice had used her social work contacts to find John a good foster home.

That evening when John returned to the hostel, Rich told him that the social worker had found him a good foster home. John looked angry: he said he hated the social worker because he believed that she controlled his father's life. He added that his head buzzed badly anytime he was supposed to talk to her. He guessed, however, that he was pleased about the foster home. He certainly didn't want to go back to live with his father. Although Rich detected a certain air of bravado in John's words, he let it pass, figuring that since John couldn't stay at Sanctuary forever, the foster home, which sounded excellent, was the only alternative.

John moved out to Lowell to his foster home, and called up Rich to tell him that he was fine and that he could come out and visit him. He did so and met John's foster parents, who seemed very warm, friendly, and open to John's needs for independence. Still, in a month, John called up to say he had persuaded his father to take him back and now he was at home again. A couple of months later, the police came by looking for John, whom we hadn't heard from since he had returned home. Later that week, the social worker called to say that John had been picked up in Pennsylvania, had gone to court, and had been released in his father's custody. John called to tell us of his adventure. He had left again in the midst of a fight with his father, and again his father had sworn not to take him back. John eventually persuaded him to, however, and pleaded in court to be released to his father.

The staff was partly confused while dealing face-to-face with John. From his description of his home situation, and especially from the social worker's, it seemed that Sanctuary's role should be to support him in his attempts to break away. John didn't really want to leave home permanently, however, as became clear after awhile. He needed to run away to get some distance on the relationship and from his father. John felt that he was not being permitted to live his own life. A father and son living alone can become very close, and that closeness can be smothering to an adolescent trying to define his own identity, even though this intimacy is also something special. John needed to test his father's feelings for him and the running-away cycle offered him that chance. After being made incredibly angry by John's running away, the father was forced to retreat into saying, in effect, "I want you back—I love you."

Sanctuary provided a safe and friendly place for John to run *to* while working things out with his father. Because he felt that he could not trust the social worker, it was important that John believe he could trust Rich. The counselor was in a good position. Unlike the social worker, he had no connections with John's father or their past, but he was aware of all these factors. He was able to be supportive, furthermore, of both his running away and also of his returning to his father.

WHEN YOU CAN'T GO HOME AGAIN

In contrast to runaways like Fran, Susie, Billy, and John, who all ended up back at home or planned to return, is a category of runaways who truly do not have a home in any human sense of the word to go back to. These runaways struggle to escape from objectively unlivable home situations to find environments where it is possible for them to grow, and love, and have a little self-respect. Ann, Tina, and Dave are examples of kids who are running hard in order to get to a place where they have a chance to live and have a little peace.

Ann

Ann's parents had been divorced. Since neither of them wanted her, her uncle had legal custody of her, and she had lived with him in Chelsea ever since she was thirteen. She was sixteen when she came to Sanctuary in the midst of a large group of other kids. She had dark hair, blue eyes, and was tall, heavy, and slightly awkward. The counselors did not find out anything about her until a few nights later when they had to go down to the police station to bail her out for shoplifting. At the station she was understandably frightened and disoriented. She was released that night, and the counselors spent a good deal of time with her in the week before her trial date.

Ann told her counselor that she had been kicked out of high school for being absent all the time and was now training to be a nurse's aid. She had left her uncle's home, she said, because she was so lonely there, and had come to Harvard Square to find friends. She complained that for the past year her uncle almost never spoke to her: after he came home from work, he drank beer and watched television, except when he went straight from work to the bar. She said she thought that he neither cared very deeply about her nor would miss her if she left, so she had run away.

Ann went by the name "Flip" among kids in the Square because she liked to appear more crazy than she really was. The counselors thought that she was, in fact, not *that* freaky, just lonely, seeking attention, and even willing to get caught by the police over a petty crime so that someone would be forced to take care of her. Ann seemed to be experiencing many emotions with which she didn't know how to deal. She laughed a lot, often inappropriately, and smoked cigarettes continuously.

Ann's counselor also met her uncle during the days before she went to court. He was a pleasant, bewildered man who thought that Ann, having run away and hung around in the Square with all those "hippies," should simply be locked up in a mental hospital. The counselor worked hard at convincing the uncle that the girl was not insane; after the counselor forced the uncle and niece to talk together for a brief time, the uncle withdrew his demand that Ann be locked up. The uncle added one new insight to the situation: Ann had run away shortly after her annual visit to her parents, which the law required.

Several counselors went to court with Ann. They argued with the judge for a placement in a halfway house or therapeutic commune. The judge agreed that Ann shouldn't go back to her uncle and said that he was open to new ideas for a home for her. This case represents a landmark for Sanctuary: for the first time the court awarded custody of a minor to the organization if it could provide a long-term place for her to live. During this period the staff had been trying to fund and set up a therapeutic commune; they thought it might be ready for occupancy in a short time. When the Sanctuary commune failed to materialize, however, and no suitable foster home could be found, Ann was sent to live with her brother and his wife in a town outside of Boston.

Ann had intense feelings of rejection, not surprising considering her parents' treatment of her. The tensions and agony entailed in attempting to have polite visits with each of her parents seem to have prompted her to leave her barren life with her uncle. It was also clear, to both the court and the counselors, that Ann was neither insane by any definition nor a particularly "bad" girl; she simply had no home. Matching Ann up with her brother and sister-in-law was just a holding action; although she liked her brother, she was tense around his wife, and everyone thought of the arrangment as one that would end when Ann became eighteen and could move out on her own. Operating from that base, however, she would be able to continue her nurse's aid training—if the other factors in her life remain stable enough.

Tina

When Tina from Savannah, Georgia, was born, her sixteen-year-old mother painfully decided that she was too immature to raise the infant. For this reason Tina lived with her mother's elderly parents till the death of her grandmother when Tina was fourteen. By that time the mother had married, was raising two young children, and had enough money to support the girl. So Tina went to live with her for the first time.

Tina's counselor, Elizabeth, reports that "from the way Tina's mother described the girl's lonely upbringing, I could tell that she had tremendous feelings of guilt about not having kept her daughter with her." She added that "Tina, too, had trouble talking about the fact that her mother had not kept her; when she mentioned her mother, it was always with anger and scorn in her voice."

For six months Tina remained with her mother's new family. Although there were few outbreaks of hostility between mother and daughter, the relationship was in fact tense and distant. One problem was that her mother simply had to devote a great deal of her attention to her young sons and her husband. She tried to be warm and loving to Tina but could not live up to the girl's idealized expectations of what living at home would be like. Finally Tina left home and spent about five months hitchhiking around the country, passing herself off as eighteen years old. She looked old enough to get away with it since her body was developed and her face did not give her away.

A few days after she arrived in Boston she came to Sanctuary. She was a strikingly healthy looking street kid with clear skin, bright blue eyes, and clean hair wrapped in a braid around her head. Her travel stories and her apparent self-assurance attracted both the counselors and the other kids. Her self-sufficient stance ceased to awe the staff, however, as they got to know Tina better. Behind the charisma was a lonely little girl. No matter how many kids surrounded her, she did not have real relationships with them, either with the men or the women. Her wandering around the streets at night began to seem not like bravery but a kind of helpless indifference to her own safety.

Elizabeth, one of the counselors who had taken a special interest in Tina, wanted to help her find a home which would be happy and supportive. She hoped that Tina would be able to stop running, perhaps to try therapy, and attend a progressive high school. Elizabeth hoped to find Tina a place where she would get encouragement for the free, creative, and constructive parts of her personality.

Briefly things looked promising. Elizabeth talked at length with Tina's mother by telephone, and she agreed to let Tina try living in a foster home if Elizabeth could find a good one. She was very reluctant to give up her daughter so soon after they had been reunited but realized that the demands of her new family made it impossible for her to meet all of Tina's needs. Elizabeth talked to the parents of a Sanctuary staff member who lived in Cambridge and were willing to try to work with Tina; in recognition of her extensive street experience, they would try to respect her freedom and at the same time give her both limits and warmth. When Tina moved in, her new parents asked her only to check in at home every day until school started, when they would all figure out the best possible arrangments. But Tina immediately began disappearing for two or three days at a time, taking lots of drugs, and getting picked up by the police for loitering.

Tina's foster family, the Morgans, became upset about their legal responsibility, fearing that Tina's mother could sue them for negligence if she became aware of her daughter's illegal activities. Elizabeth confronted Tina with this problem, pointing out that this was her last chance for a secure and warm home environment. Tina tossed her head at the words *warmth* and *security,* saying that she would rather live on the streets. Although Elizabeth felt as if she were letting Tina down by taking her home, she had to do it.

Finally, the counselor drove Tina back to Georgia. Elizabeth felt discouraged that the arrangement with the foster home had not worked out and was fearful that living at home would not turn out any better for Tina. Her fears proved to be justified. Tina seemed unable to overcome her feelings of rejection, and her mother felt at a loss in trying to cope with a daughter who was such a puzzling amalgam of self-sufficient adult and frightened child.

During the three months following her return home Tina frequently stayed out at night, left school early or did not bother to go at all, and had numerous episodes of heavy drug-taking. Finally she left home again, but was picked up by the police trying to hitchhike out of town. She was taken to juvenile court as a runaway. Her mother, concerned with the harmful influence which a reform school might exert on Tina, persuaded the judge to commit her to a mental hospital. After a few weeks Tina wrote to Elizabeth that confinement was dragging her down. She felt that she could not communicate with the other patients or the staff.

The key factor which motivated Tina's leaving home was apparently her powerful feelings of being rejected by her mother through her childhood, and the sudden appearance of her mother's new family. As Elizabeth stated, Tina's deep-seated belief that her mother did not love her—why else did she send her away?—was one of the girl's very strongest emotions. It seems a wonder that she managed to live with her mother in relative peace, even if not in harmony. Her careless wanderings around the city at night represent something deeper than an indifference to her own safety—almost as if she were being so "wild" and "free" to force her mother, or the counselor in her place, to intervene on her behalf. Her recklessness might even have been motivated by a desire to punish the mother: if she were injured in the course of her travels, it would have been the mother's fault for allowing her to run away, just as the mother had permitted her to live apart for so many years.

In considering both these factors, but especially the competition posed by the new family, it is important to remember that Tina was at this time coming to grips with her physical maturity as a woman, and all the issues that entails. Her relatively new relationship with her mother was precarious anyway; having another family claim a good part of the mother's time and emotions proved unmanageable for the girl. It was especially difficult for Tina because she had no previous, stable relationship with her mother to rely on as a basis of trust, though she had yearned for such a relationship and had hoped to find it when her mother took her back.

Once Tina had left and had been brought back, it is understandable that there would be problems in her settling down in the same home again. She had been on the road for five months, had managed her own life, and had gone wherever she wanted to. She had experimented with drugs and sex, and they had become, albeit prematurely, familiar aspects of her life. On one level, she believed that she had proven that she could take care of herself; how could she then submit herself to the limits which are usually imposed on the life of a sixteen-year-old girl in her small home town? We are not saying that the limits are invalid; perhaps it would have been better for her if she had more limits to abide by. The point is, however, that given her experiences on the road, it would have been extremely difficult to settle down in a conservative setting even if her home situation had been better.

Concerning placing Tina with the Morgans, Elizabeth stated: "I guess I was really rushing things. I sensed she would never stay in a conventional home. I thought she would be able to ease herself back into the idea of living in a family by staying with the Morgans who would combine freedom with some limits and who would show her that they cared about her. But Tina was not at the point where she could handle any parent-figure caring for her or 'controlling' her." Tina also may have in some ways construed the freedom which the Morgans allowed her as simply another device to be rid of her.

It seems possible, though not likely, that a more strict, though still warm and loving atmosphere would have been better for Tina. She might have construed the discipline as signifying more concern, but it seems highly unlikely that she would have put herself in a position where she again would have risked rejection, this time by the foster family. Keeping in mind the freedom she had become accustomed to on the streets, Elizabeth strongly believed that Tina simply would not have tolerated this kind of environment. It remains a real possibility that Tina needed limits, and that an atmosphere with strong discipline softened by love would have been better.

Maybe some kind of commune or therapeutic halfway house would have been appropriate, though it is hard to see how she would have been able to keep up her end of the responsibilities entailed in living in this kind of environment. Any fate, however, would probably have been better for Tina than incarceration in a mental hospital, next to which the dangers involved in being on the road seem inconsequential. Two important lessons about counseling runaways came out of the case. In ways Elizabeth had put her own conception of what Tina was and what she needed in place of what the girl actually was: "something more drastic than the arrangement with the Morgans was necessary, although it is unclear what the counselor could have found that would have worked better. The second lesson is more disheartening: despite a counselor's willingness to do anything possible, it will not always be within her power to help some kids.

Dave

The tension between Dave and his stepfather made his life miserable. His attempts to get himself into a healthier environment were thwarted by his parents, who were backed up by the legal system. To quote a popular song, Dave "fought the law and the law won."

His face covered with fresh bruises, Dave came into the storefront one day in early September. He was from Worcester, Massachusetts, thirteen years old, and small for his age. He had inherited the very black skin of his father, though his mother was white. After he had skipped his grocery store job earlier that week, he said, his white stepfather had beaten him up. Dave told Stu, his counselor, that his father was "a real bastard" who beat him up regularly, and that he wasn't going to stand it anymore. He neither would say any more about it nor let Stu call his parents to get permission for him to stay overnight. Although he seemed frightened, his stance was mainly tough and determined.

Dave explained that a friend in Worcester had found him a ride as far as Boston. He did not have enough money to go any further and was afraid that the police would pick him up if he tried hitchhiking, so he had come to Sanctuary hoping to find help in getting to his aunt's home in Maine. He had lived with her when he was a very young child and had spent this past summer with her; he said that she would definitely let him stay with her. The aunt had in fact offered to keep him all year, but his parents had refused, saying it just wasn't "right." Although he had only been home for a month, he had already twice tried hitchhiking back to Maine, only to get picked up both times before he got out of Massachusetts.

From the storefront Dave called his aunt, who agreed to get on a bus and come pick him up. While Dave was using another phone to get bus schedules, Stu talked to the aunt privately. Crying while she talked, she explained that Dave was the child of her sister's first marriage, which, obviously, had been to a black man; the marriage had ended before Dave was born. The stepfather hated the fact that the boy was black, she said, because he felt it represented his wife's "immoral" past. The aunt said that there had always been tensions in the family around Dave; she personally had seen the stepfather push the boy down a flight of stairs. She was not sure why his parents refused to consider the boy's living with her except that she did not get along well with the stepfather, who had once called her a "nigger-loving old maid."

The aunt arrived late the next day and took Dave with her. Looking kindly and nervous, she thanked Stu and said she would call Sanctuary when they returned to Bangor. Dave called three days later to say that he was well and happy and would be starting school in a couple of days.

Stu did not hear anything from or about Dave until a month later when Dave came into the storefront with a friend, announcing that he could only stay a few minutes because he had a stolen car waiting outside. He quickly told Stu what had happened to make him return to the area. On the third day he was at school in Maine the state troopers had picked him up in his classroom and taken him to the airport where his parents were waiting to take him home again. Dave's aunt had been unaware that by filing for custody of the child, she might at least have delayed his return home while court hearings proceeded and might possibly have been awarded legal guardianship of the boy. His stepfather had threatened to sue the aunt for contributing to the delinquency of a minor, but his mother had persuaded him not to. Dave said he himself was finally put on probation for "stubborn child" charges.

Dave added that during the time he had been home, his stepfather had been worse than ever and that he was now splitting again. He planned to steal cars all the way to Canada; he knew he could not try Maine again because that would be the first place his parents would look. At a loss as to what to tell Dave, Stu started to tell him a little about the dangers of ending up in reform school, but he and his friend couldn't stay to listen and headed out the door. Later that night, however, Dave called to say that he had changed his mind about Canada and was back in Worcester.

Stu thought that, even though Dave did not get caught that time, he certainly would get in serious trouble eventually. He had a whole gang of friends who were well on their way into urban crime. They talked very knowingly about breaking and entering stores, as well as stealing cars.

It is revealing that although Dave had a strong group of friends to be a part of, he still sincerely wanted the relatively less exciting life his aunt's home offered. She was a rather proper, conservative lady who was firm with Dave, which he knew from his experiences living with her. It did not seem as if Dave was planning to "con" her in any way. Stu and the other counselors felt that they could really trust Dave's attempts to get to Maine as a serious search for a healthy home to grow up in. It seems natural for a kid living in a house with as much conflict and cruelty as Dave's to need to get out of the environment. Dave was fortunate in having a stable alternative, an aunt to go to who was willing to have him and whom he respected and loved. But the law punishes kids for running away from their parents. In an attempt to find a decent alternative, Dave was punished with probation and the other social effects of criminalization of a thirteen-year-old boy. And he's still at home.

In cases like Dave's, with the kids under eighteen, a forest of legal hassles spring up both for the runaway and the counselor. It is against the law for children to run away, but it is highly unclear what the law means by the term "runaway." In Massachusetts, for example, the law has never defined the term, which is listed in the section (Chap. 272, sec. 53) which deals with "stubborn children" and "common nightwalkers" (prostitutes). Does running away mean leaving home without parent's permission? Without parents' knowledge? Is it running around the block or outside the city limits or across state lines? Is it being gone overnight? Twenty-four hours? A week? Do the kid's reasons for running away have any bearing on whether or not she can be prosecuted as a "runaway?"

The Massachusetts Supreme Court has passed two rulings on the term "stubborn children". In the case of Joyner vs. Commonwealth, decided in July, 1970, the court found the defendent innocent because she was over 18 and, therefore, "not a child." The court's opinion indicates that only "juveniles" (those under 17 years of age) can be prosecuted as "stubborn children". In a more recent case Brasher vs. Commonwealth, decided in spring, 1971, the court defined a stubborn child as a juvenile who persistently disobeys the lawful and reasonable commands of her parents or guardians. It had been hoped that the court would rule that the entire statute, which includes both "runaways" and "stubborn children," was unconstitutional, but this was unfortunately not the case.

As it is now, police must serve the "stubborn child" warrants that parents write out. Police can and do arrest young-looking kids they suspect of being runaways. The police of a different state will hold a kid if the police from the parents' state request it. This usually happens only when parents have a definite idea of which state in which to look, as in Dave's case. Then the parents come pick up the kid. The kid who refuses to go home before trial is kept in a juvenile detention center until the court date.

The runaway sometimes has counsel, sometimes doesn't, although she is advised of her right to counsel. She often ends up with her parents' lawyer, and her parents are present at her trial where they hear all the testimony a kid is brave enough to offer against them. If an underage kid is caught doing anything else illegal or of questionable legality–shoplifting, loitering, panhandling, hitchhiking–she is sent home and often charged.

The human costs of criminalization of runaways are tremendous. The law seems to be set up first to keep families together at whatever costs to the individuals, and second to keep kids from taking independent actions. The problem of an entire family becomes a legal issue where only one member of a family, the child, is charged. Bringing a runaway to trial means that blame must be determined, which is the least useful way of talking about the reasons why a kid runs away or of trying to deal with the crises brought to the surface by the action. Legal processes can become a way for the other family members to avoid their share of responsibility. The least powerful party under the law, the kid, may be charged and punished or returned to the same home which he felt he had to leave in the first place. Kids are thus told that they're delinquent for something which isn't their "fault." The customary solutions are guaranteed to exacerbate the problems–sending a kid either back to her home or to reform school, where she will certainly become delinquent if her home hasn't made her so already. As widespread a social problem as running away must not be allowed to remain solely under legal jurisdiction. What should be legally recognized are the reasons why kids sometimes *can't* live in their homes, situations which may cause kids much more harm than the act of running away. Dave's story is a case in point.

Some judges and probation officers are sensitive to the problems. As judges gain increasing experience with runaways, they are beginning to see the shortsightedness of sending the kids who keep running away back to their homes and are more open to alternate solutions. The judges who saw Ann and Windy in court were willing to try situations other than the home or state institutions. During the summer several probation officers used the hostel as lodging for kids they were working with. We feel hopeful that if we had the proper facilities and staff, the courts would be willing to give the Sanctuary longer custody of kids.

Individual communities might well set up houses where kids could go when they were having trouble at home. Kids need a place to talk to counselors and other runaways about what is going on without having to leave their friends and school. Their parents could be notified of their whereabouts but be unable to take them away for a specified period of time—perhaps two weeks. Even then they should not do so without family therapy sessions in which the kid's reasons for running were evaluated seriously and alternatives were considered. It should be made legal for juveniles to come to agencies like Sanctuary, either to try to work things out so that they can go home stronger and more independent, or, in certain instances, to set up procedures to leave home for longer periods of time, or even permanently.

Counseling runaways falls under the charge of "contributing to the delinquency of a minor," another fuzzy classification. Do you have to *intend* your actions to lead the child into delinquency to be guilty? What kinds of actions are defined as contributing to her delinquency? talking sympathetically to a runaway? not calling the police the minute a runaway walks in the door? permitting a runaway to sleep overnight in a hostel? allowing a runaway to stay overnight talking about the problems? Places like Sanctuary must continue to operate despite vagueness of the law. The staff tries to stretch the letter of the law as much as possible and accept the fact that a few court cases may arise. The staff follows a general rule of counseling runaways as much as the kids want, discussing with them all possible alternatives. We refrain from taking any positive actions connected with kids' running away and require parental permission for kids to stay overnight with us. The irony of this policy is apparent: we have to send a thirteen-year-old runaway who feels she can't call home out to the street to find a place to sleep.

Since most of the kids are underage, counselors feel that they simply have to take all the risks with the law that they can afford to in order to be of any help at all to the kids who need them the most. Since it opened Sanctuary has been negotiating with the Cambridge police force to arrange a "grace period" of twenty-four hours to give more time to make contact with a kid before she has to call her parents or go out on the streets. This hasn't been arranged yet, however. Whenever the police come with a warrant for a kid, the counselors have no choice but to help them look around the storefront or hostel. They do not call the police, except occasionally to help a kid determine her legal status.

Antiquated laws, inadequate resources, and sometimes parents limit what Sanctuary can do with kids. Our job is to push those limits as far as we can and to remain aware of our own fantasies about the kids as well as the kids' expectations of what they can get from us.

CHANGING INSIDE

Many of the kids who came to Sanctuary were going through a lonely and often painful time of change. They were not always stereotypical street people, but in some real sense they were on the street: uprooted, trying to break with their pasts and searching hard to figure out who they were and where they were going. As they struggled they seemed disoriented and confused and very vulnerable.

The three young people who are described in this chapter were all in the midst of intense self-examination and change. In being with them and trying to help them the counselors found that it was important to offer something of themselves as individuals, but at the same time to clarify the role to which they were willing to commit themselves in the relationship. They also found that it was crucial to the process to allow whomever they were counseling enough space to define herself.

Marlene

Quite often, counseling at Sanctuary focuses on sexual confusions, doubts, and embarrassments. A frequent example is the homosexual who feels isolated and guilty over her sexual orientation. While it is very easy to say that an individual should be able to hold up her head no matter what society says, it is no easy task to do so. A few homosexuals blurted out the nature of their sexual feelings the moment they entered the counseling office. Others, like Marlene, a twenty-three-year-old secretary in a large Boston firm, had a different way of expressing themselves: they would only begin to approach the issue of homosexuality after several meetings with their counselors.

Marlene came to Sanctuary in early July because, as she told her counselor Erica, she was very lonely and badly needed someone to talk to. The young woman said that she had been drinking steadily over the last months, and now that she had stopped, her depression was once more growing intense. She said that while she slept more than eight hours a day she was always tired, and once had broken down in tears in the supermarket for no clear reason. Erica tried to find out if anything traumatic had happened to the woman in the recent past, but Marlene just said that she had moved to Boston not too long before, had few friends, and was "just depressed." The two women talked about loneliness and other topics for more than an hour; at the end of the session Marlene said that she wanted to be able to come to the counseling center on a fairly regular basis for a few weeks to see if talking to Erica would help matters.

After that the two women met at the storefront and spent a lot of time together: talking for hours, strolling through Cambridge, and taking photographs together. Erica found Marlene very sensitive and intelligent; she said that she sincerely enjoyed being with her, and she learned a lot about taking pictures. Both Marlene's parents were artists, and she had real talent, according to Erica, in form and drawing.

Eventually Marlene and Erica were on comfortable enough terms that Marlene was able to open some of her problems to Erica. It was obviously hard for Marlene to talk about her homosexual life, but one day when they were together and a little drunk, Marlene explained that she had originally come to Boston because she wanted to be near a certain woman with whom she had been having an affair. Recently, this woman had left Marlene for another woman. Erica wanted to support Marlene, but was unsure of how to do it, so she tentatively asked about the relationship: "Was it painful? Were you very upset by it?" Marlene said yes quietly, but the conversation then moved on to something else. She and Marlene continued to hang around together, to do things together.

Erica had thought a great deal about her own response to homosexuality, trying to struggle with her own socialization which condemns relationships between people of the same sex. Although she did not know any homosexual women very well, she did have a few acquaintances who were gay; and she had comfortable, nonthreatening relationships with them. She tried to be honest with Marlene regarding her own, mainly heterosexual, orientation. One day on a walk Erica said that she wanted to tell Marlene that she had never had experiences with women, only with men, and that she wasn't sure she completely understood female homosexuality. Marlene responded by saying that she had been with men also, but that it was just easier with women, that women were more tender. Erica felt good that she and Marlene had been able to talk about their differences in experience and direction without threatening the relationship. Erica was able to say that she wasn't interested in the possibilities of sexual interaction between them, and at the same time she found that by giving Marlene her support, respect, friendship, and plain *company*, she was giving Marlene the human comfort she needed.

Erica wondered whether the isolation caused by Marlene's sexual preference for women might not be a deep source of loneliness to her. Erica said that at first she was not at all sure that Marlene had come to talk because she was homesexual; but, she adds, she had thought of this possibility because the girl had so often mentioned her former lover in the course of the conversation. It seems likely that she was suffering from extreme loneliness for several reasons. Marlene was in a common situation among young men and women today: she was alone in the city. She had come to Boston with the hope of being with someone she loved. This had not worked out. Not only did she have to cope with the grief which this breakup caused her, but she was faced with the necessity of coping alone, in a strange city, without the support of friends. In a deeper way, because society in general offers condemnation instead of support for homosexual love, she could not expect to talk about her troubles even to a sympathetic acquaintance. If she had tried to explain her problems to people in the office she probably would have been fired.

In trying to help Marlene to a happier situation, Erica approached her homosexuality very tentatively, after considerable contact which encouraged Marlene to feel comfortable and secure. The counselor did not limit the extent of the relationship to the problems entailed in Marlene's being a lesbian. She furthermore did not feel obligated to instruct Marlene not to feel "bad" about her homosexuality. This is as useless as it is insensitive: it does not make a homosexual feel better to be told this by a heterosexual who does not daily have to face the burden of society's disapproval, nor does it meet the problems she encounters in leading her life in any concrete way. Erica considered suggesting that Marlene join Gay Womens Liberation, but concluded that this was a decision the woman should make when and if she wanted.

She tried to sense whether Marlene was sure that she did not want to try to love men, sexually and otherwise, and finally asked directly if that were the case. Marlene replied that she felt no impulse to have relationships with men. At that point Erica gave up the idea of a psychiatric referral for Marlene. The counselor did mention that she herself had had good experience with a psychiatrist, implying that that was a possible mode of action if Marlene wished it; but Marlene showed no interest. Erica knew a psychiatrist might be useful in helping an individual get over fears or other problems standing in the way of a form of sexual activity she desired; but since what Marlene wanted was not to become heterosexual but to live with herself as she was, Erica believed she should not pressure Marlene into therapy. In our society how an individual handles her sexuality is a crucial factor in determining whether or not she will be "happy" in living. Yet little time has been given to basic psychological study of female homosexuality, the possible steps to self-adjustment and happiness. Beyond this is the question of how much the lesbian might be expected to adjust to normal society, and how much the society needs to adjust its mores to include the lesbian. Erica chose to deal with Marlene's loneliness and sense of being lost, something real to both women, whether or not it was intensified or caused by homosexuality in Marlene's case. At the end of the summer Marlene left Boston to find a better job in New York. Erica has received a few postcards from her, but has not heard from her for several months.

Isolation is one of the more painful problems for a woman who is gay. She tends to feel that society cannot understand her and accept her as a whole person. The problems and joys that are part of her life as a homosexual are almost never talked or written about. Even emphasis in psychiatric therapy dealing with female homosexuality is upon its deviance from the rest of society. For these reasons the gay woman often has no means for understanding and articulating her identity to herself. No matter where she looks in the social and cultural patterns which prevail today, the answer to her question, "Who am I?" is a simply a blank.

On one occasion when Marlene and Erica were walking around the viewing platform of a skyscraper at night, Marlene started free-associating on the lights and forms of the cityscape spread below. She was honestly amazed when Erica could follow what she was talking about and sometimes agreed that the lights reminded her of the same things; she was surprised that Erica understood her when she expressed her own feelings and ideas about the way the world looked. It seems possible that she had some doubt that even these dimensions of her personal experience were communicable to others–dimensions which are generally accepted as simply a part of all human experience. For a lesbian, real isolation is complicated by the inability to find ways to identify and define herself and to relate to some kind of social reality. In Marlene's case, her problems seemed to go beyond her loneliness; she felt a real and painful lack of belonging.

In most cities, including Boston, various groups and homophile organizations exist which try to ease the problem by offering mutual support and a sense of community. This kind of getting together ranges from idle conversation in a relaxed atmosphere away from social pressures, to talk groups, parties, and social actions aimed at achieving greater freedom for homosexuals in the mainstream of society. A few magazines, newspapers, and other publications devoted to homosexual experience also contribute to relieving isolation and to forming a subculture to which she can belong. Erica might have suggested these existing channels to Marlene as possible ways to help her handle her homosexuality more fully. Perhaps she would have stayed in Boston had she become involved here. As it was, she returned to New York where she had friends and began working as a librarian. Erica did not alter Marlene's life greatly; she only diminished her loneliness. She was a friend when Marlene needed a friend, and this seems to have been for both of them the important part of their interaction.

It is undeniable that, if Marlene lived in a society where homosexuality was more permissable, then she would have been experiencing far fewer internal conflicts. It is interesting to speculate about the nature of a society which outlaws love between two members of the same sex, but at the same time sanctions mutual economic exploitation. In a society which experiences—and initiates—as much violence and brutality as ours does, any love which exists should be encouraged, not outlawed. Acceptance and understanding of the forms that love can take can only enrich our sense of ourselves.

Stephanie

Jason was in the middle of an intense discussion with a friend from Seattle when Stephanie walked in. Looking about seventeen years old, she had a high, very anxious voice. She seemed to be strung out on psychedelic drugs, mistrustful, and overwhelmed with a sense of her own uselessness. Later Jason learned that her current state had been triggered by a blowup with her boyfriend about two weeks before; since then, she had done acid every day.

She said she was very lonely and felt intensely separated from her friends, and she believed that she was going to stay that way forever. It seemed that Stephanie had mentally walled herself off from all personal contacts. All the other kids in the storefront tried to be friends with her, but she never allowed them to get past the acquaintance stage; if one did start to talk to her and then moved away for any reason, she took it as a pointed rejection, especially if the acquaintance had been male.

Three days later she walked in heavily tripping on acid and talked in bizarre images and symbols all night. Jason tried to talk to her, but it turned out to be a marathon of noncommunication. Stephanie's long, straight hair seemed to bother her immensely, and she pulled on it all the time. She speculated about suicide–half to herself, half for Jason's consumption–but never got to the point where she could concretely discuss what was wrong. She was waiting for Jason to pull it all together for her, to explain everything, which he said he could not do. The next morning, about an hour before Jason's shift was over, she began rapping with a boy who was being nice to her. Jason left without saying goodbye, satisfied that she was finally getting involved with someone.

Later that morning Stephanie called Jason to say goodbye. She was being mysterious, again threatening suicide, implying that he had rejected her. Jason started to argue with her, she yelled at him, saying that he did not even care about her, that talking to her was just his job. She focused on the fact that he had left without saying goodbye. They talked about that and about her impression of him as a potential boyfriend. The counselor tried to be very honest with her about what her expectations could be: Jason explained that he was an older friend who cared about what happened to her and would like to help if this turned out to be possible.

Getting that tension out in the open seemed to allow Stephanie to start talking about the things that were really frightening and depressing her; for the first time she discussed her family. Her father had been in and out of mental hospitals; her mother had to work most of the time and rarely had a minute to spend with Stephanie. Stephanie felt that in order to grow up she had to leave her home, but she was terrified of doing this. She was very confused about her feelings toward her parents: she was torn between her loyalty to each of them, and simultaneously her feeling that they did not love her. When she spoke of suicide, it was always in terms of how much it would hurt her parents.

Jason then told her that she could leave home by finding a job and an apartment in Boston: since she had her parents' permission, she could break away. When the pair met at the storefront a week later, Stephanie was elated; she had not done drugs during the interim, and this was a record for her. She had also found herself a place in an apartment with other young people, not in Boston where the rents were too high, but in Medford, a suburb. She tried living with a group for two months–and also managed to avoid taking acid–but for various reasons decided eventually that it was not her "scene."

Stephanie informed Jason that she now wanted to be practical, to return home and get her high school diploma. They talked for some length about how her home would probably be no different than before. She has been back to Sanctuary periodically over the year. Life is not easy for her. Her parents are still absorbed in their own dilemnas, and her home life is indeed as bad as before. She had worked hard at school, but had not been able to graduate because she had missed a whole year of gym, which was essential for the diploma. Occasionally she would fall back into taking many drugs, but so far she has always pulled herself out of such periods. She is now trying to make enough money so that she can travel across the country.

Initially, while Stephanie was tripping, Jason recognized a need, request, or expectation for him to "pull it all together" for her, which he resisted. Then, shortly, Stephanie's fantasy of counselor-as-boyfriend surfaced; Jason punctured that fantasy, and in so doing identified the role he was equipped to play in a relationship with Stephanie–that of an "older friend who cared." A significant change in Stephanie's attitude toward her problems occured after she began speaking about the home situation she wants to leave: Stephanie was receptive to his encouragement in a way she wouldn't have been previously. Together they undertook apartment and job hunting. Finally, Stephanie has returned intermittently to keep Jason posted on how she's progressing. By now their relationship seems much less personal; Stephanie is independent of Jason as well as of her parents. Regardless of how accurately Jason assessed Stephanie's long-term problems, the sequence of adjustments which each made in relating to the other could only have been valuable. Their interaction stimulated a willingness to confide in each other and, as respect and trust grew between them, Jason was required to speak directly to the expectations he sensed in Stephanie; her willingness to keep Jason up-to-date over the following period of months suggests a mutual expectation of warm and long-term contact.

At first contact Jason consciously restricted his own expectations of who he could be for Stephanie while she was tripping. "She was waiting for us to pull it all together, which, of course, we couldn't do," he said. However, we respect his refusal to make sense of someone else's trip; there is a thin line between this and "laying a line on someone"—a hardly-to-be-respected counseling strategy. Perhaps, Stephanie understood his decision not to pretend that it was possible for him to pull her trip together. She seems to have returned his respect for her by fantasizing about him. Who is to say whether Stephanie's anger about Jason's not saying goodnight is the anger of a rejected lover or the pique of someone who, in her loneliness, refuses to allow a potential contact to drift out of her life? Or perhaps it is the resentment of someone who senses a hypocrisy in the concept of nine-to-five counseling compassion; Stephanie's saying that talking to her was just his job suggests this last possibility. In any case, as soon as Jason responded to her anger, as soon as he outlined to Stephanie how he understood his relationship to her, he made their relationship less ambiguous and impersonal. Stephanie for the first time knew that Jason wanted her to think of him as an "older friend," and if she was disappointed that he didn't want her to think of him as a potential lover, she knew at least that he did want her to think of him.

From this newly explicit basis of understanding, Stephanie felt secure enough with Jason to begin to talk about her family and her desire to leave them. Perhaps Stephanie's sense of encouragement about leaving home was directly a function of her feeling supported by Jason and able to expect that support to continue. If so, then Stephanie's decision to leave home was largely a result of her pushing Jason to clarify his relation to her in the "lover or old friend" episode. Manipulative responses by clients are often met by manipulative approaches by counselors: there can be nothing less manipulative, however, than Jason's speaking seriously and respectfully to Stephanie, telling her that he would not allow her to consider him her boyfriend.

Moreover, Jason's willingness to respect Stephanie's perceptions (of him as lover) enough to discuss them openly, to take them into account, grounded their relationship at the nonmanipulative level of decent human interaction. Jason could have chosen to dismiss Stephanie's anger as inappropriate to a counselor-client relationship; had he done so, he would have given a forceful signal that he intended to relate to Stephanie in an ambiguously professional manner. Instead, his willingness to level with Stephanie about his personal response to her clarified the role which he was willing to fulfill in their interaction.

It comes as a relief to the client when the counselor is willing to clearly spell out the status of their relatedness. Paradoxically, placing explicit limits on a counseling interaction helps create the trust, relief, and self-recognition that makes possible a fuller interaction. The paradox is a reflection on conventional therapeutic interactions in which the counselor's personal responses are regarded as inappropriate; it is small wonder that so often the client's attempts to connect with these feelings on the counselor's part are regarded as manipulation, when in essence the counselor is being fully as manipulative. Stephanie's case is instructive in suggesting that this whole issue of manipulation can be handled honestly and directly by limiting the counseling interaction when feeling between counselor and client require this clarification.

BAD TRIPS

Many kids use drugs out of a desire for self-exploration, for relaxation, or just for fun. Others use drugs in working out self-destructive drives or to attempt to blot out reality altogether. In general, young people take drugs for many of the same reasons the older generation drinks alcohol: to be sociable and to remove themselves temporarily from stressful situations. Drug use on the streets may be quite different from that on a campus, where drugs are usually taken in a reasonably sane manner within a protective environment.

The drug use of those who come to Sanctuary often involves many personal issues and unresolved conflicts. As sometimes happens, a young person may take drugs to the extent that she cannot function in the world, or that she endangers her own emotional or physical well-being. In these cases, of course, drugs are a serious problem. The question becomes crucial when heroin, amphetamines, or barbiturates are involved. The Sanctuary counselors, however, do not perceive drugs per se as the major problem in the lives of these kids, although enabling a young person to cease a pattern of self-destructive drug use can sometimes improve the situation. But this is not an answer. Even if a counselor could get a troubled young person into a drug-free environment, the person would not necessarily have solved all her conflicts or be happy.

The staff has usually found that drugs are usually not the cause of the kid's basic problem but symptomatic of those conflicts. It is, therefore, important to examine what drug use expresses in the context of the person's whole life.

The biggest difference between the use of drugs on the streets and on the campus is illustrated by the fact that for the past year "downs," the street name for barbiturates or tranquilizers, have become the most frequently used drugs by members of the street culture; college students rarely take sleeping pills as an escape. These drugs, by the way, also are the most popular in suburbia today; they are liberally prescribed by psychiatrists and other doctors. Downs are associated more than any other group of drugs with self-destructive behavior. Unlike most of the other frequently used drugs, such as marihuana, downs are used to deaden one's sense of the world, one's sense of self. And although most young people use LSD to explore themselves or to try to see their lives from different perspectives, repeated, large doses of LSD can be, and on the street often are, used for the same purpose—not to break down barriers to communication, but to erect high walls between the individual and others and also to shield the individual against overly demanding situations.

Sanctuary counselors and teachers have consistently found that acid begins to cause trouble when it is used by kids who have nothing else in their life to hold on to. If a young person is secure in her own competence at her work and her ability to maintain friendships, it is rare that an occasional acid trip would cause her serious problems, though there are exceptions to even this tenuous generalization. When a young person is all alone, however, unable to make connection with any meaningful pursuit or relationships, then trouble begins. Perhaps this is because acid becomes the central fact of the person's life, and she cannot build a life out of chemicals; alternatively, it is possible that people who are not securely anchored in their environment pin too much hope and too many aspirations on the acid trip, thus thinking that it will "change" them and allow them to become happy or successful. The case of Will, a nineteen-year-old from West Virginia working in Boston, is an example.

Will

At eight in the morning Stu received a call from a pyschiatrist at the City Hospital who asked him to pick up Will, who had flipped out on acid the night before and been brought into the hospital by the police. Will was still coming down from six tabs of acid and much grass and liquor and thought that everyone was after him. Stu guided him through the end of his long trip and after six hours of intensive rapping believed that Will was all right, though perhaps only for the present.

Will described his trip as a powerful one, which involved "the death" of his previous self and "a rebirth of a new person." Will had been working in a shoe factory in Boston and was confused about where he fit in between a band of worldly hippies and the group of "greasers" he worked with. He wasn't sure who his friends were, and since he spent a lot of time by himself, his friendships weren't very strong. When tripping, he was overwhelmed by the oppressive and hostile character of the back streets of South Boston; he didn't feel as if he had any power to act against all the strong forces working against him—a feeling that had basis in the objective situation. For instance, as he remained immobile in the back of his truck, someone reached in and stole his radio. He was scared about being picked up by the police and also afraid that he was letting down the friends who supplied the acid by getting them busted. He was sure that everyone was watching him and plotting against him. He was even unsure about Stu. Will had felt, probably accurately, that he had come close to seriously injuring himself while running around in the streets of South Boston.

Stu talked to Will about the things that were most on his mind. Will came to the conclusion that taking drugs was bumming out his whole life and making it harder for him to live. He asked Stu to drive him to the train station where he bought a ticket for West Virginia, where his parents and a girlfriend lived. Will talked about getting back to a familiar country environment, getting his high school equivalency certificate, and going to the state university.

Stu tried to make him slow down, but at the time he felt that this plan to return to his home was generally Will's best option. They talked about how Will had to adjust to living at home after being on his own, but Will maintained that in many ways it would be much easier. During the trip Will had been awed by the importance of communication, and he began to talk about how important it was going to be for him to keep in touch with his old friends instead of remaining such a loner.

All Stu finally knows about Will is that he boarded a train to go home; he has not heard from him since. The move might well have been the best thing for Will to do; according to Stu, any environment would have been better for Will than his lonely life in Boston. In addition, Will had not had serious conflicts with his parents; he had only wanted to experiment with being on his own. This is natural for young people; today college provides many with an opportunity to try being independent. But with Will's family's economic status, this had not been possible, so Will tried in his own way. Although at the time the decision to return home had seemed like an excellent one to both parties, Stu now agrees that given the great flux going on in Will's mind due to his trip, it might have been better to have insisted more forcefully that he give the matter more thought when he had time and was calm enough to do so. Stu also feels that his own rather idealized preference for the country life might have come through and influenced Will's decision.

Bad-trip counseling differs considerably in style from more general, longer-term counseling. A conversation between a disoriented acid bad-tripper and a stranger who is known only as a hot-line counselor poses enormous complications, particularly if the only contact is over the telephone. The kind of easy, informal contact that allows the growth of trust becomes impossible in the situation of the bad-tripper contacting Sanctuary for emotional first-aid. The sense of urgency that a tripper projects requires, first of all, an immediate, calming response to persuade her that panic will disappear when the trip is over.

The peculiar property of the psychedelic drugs, particularly for isolated and distrustful trippers, is that the user can mercilessly distinguish between truthful expressions of concern and phony cant or technique–a quality of the acid experience which hinders most conventional and unspontaneous counseling approaches. As a result, it is very difficult for an unstoned counselor and a tripping client to undertake a mutual exploration of a specific problem, to interact fully in a counseling relationship. In fact this kind of interaction may not even be desirable from the client's point of view: it may be precisely because she is speaking to a stranger that a bad-tripper is willing to make contact with a counselor at all. Feeling protected by her confusion, a tripping client may be more comfortable exposing her confusion and apprehensiveness all at once than in a two-sided counseling interaction. Moreover, given the suggestibility and defenselessness of most trippers, rarely are there mutually recognized sanctions for a focused and forceful counseling intervention during a bad trip.

Rather than endorsing either the extreme response of talking someone "down off her trip"—persuading her that she will not benefit from the process she is going through—or the equally extreme measures of talking someone through her trip, which is an eight-hour project, the counselor must respect severe limitations on how she can hope to interact with a bad-tripper. The counselor's task is to speak in straightforward, nonjudgmental language to someone who may simply be unable to understand much of what she says. She needs to be able to shift conversational gears quickly and with composure as she discovers, for example, that a remark like "it sounds like you've been having a heavy trip" gets interpreted by the client as confirmation that her trip is as agonizing as it seems with more to come.

The counselor needs to learn that quite often there is nothing to talk about with a tripping client, nothing to establish or disestablish. Her sensitivity must be directed toward reassuring tones of voice and calm conversations about nothing in particular, rather than toward content or persuasion. Finally, she needs to enjoy the conversation with a tripper as much as possible for its own sake. Without this kind of relaxed and coherent point of view, the counselor may engage herself in a conversation in which two parties compound each other's confusions while neither speaks out of an honest self-awareness.

SEPARATE AND UNEQUAL

The best statement which we have read about the position of black people in America is put forth by two black psychiatrists, William H. Grier, and Price K. Cobbs, the authors of *Black Rage*. Their description of cultural paranoia accurately characterizes an attitude of many young blacks who came through the storefront. The authors' view of the role of a good therapist is one with which we agree.

> It is necessary for a black man in America to develop a profound distrust of his white fellow citizens and of the nation. . . . For his own survival then, he must develop a *cultural paranoia* in which every white man is a potential enemy unless proved otherwise and every social system is set against him unless he personally finds out otherwise. . . . He can never quite respect laws which have no respect for him, and laws designed to protect white men are viewed as white men's laws. . . . Too much psychotherapy involves striving only for a change in the inner world and a consequent adaptation to the world outside. . . . A

> black man's soul can live only if he is oriented toward a change of the racial order. A good therapist helps a man change his inner life so that he can more effectively change his outer world. (pp. 149-151)

Black kids must struggle through the same varieties of adolescent questions as everyone else—and then some. Grier and Cobbs explain: "The black boy in growing up encounters some strange impediments. Schools discourage his ambitions, training for valued skills is not available to him, and when he does triumph in some youthful competition he receives compromised praise, not the glory he might expect. In time he comes to see that society has locked arms against him." (p. 49).

A number of black kids, mostly working-class males, hung around the storefront last summer. Their presence as marginal members of the hip street scene—black kids have had their own street scene for years—probably resulted from their exclusion elsewhere. Young blacks often do not have any particular place to belong to; many leave their families, psychically if not physically, at a very early age. Sanctuary provided less than a fully satisfying environment for them.

The counterculture is mainly a white phenomenon, and the staff expected to deal with white street kids. Counselors were surprised to find a significant number of black kids becoming Sanctuary regulars. The white kids in the storefront did not fully accept the black kids, who in turn never became fully integrated into the group dynamics of the storefront or hostel. The presence of black people was felt through sparks flying from their own interaction or from black-white conflict. The white kids related to them in an ambivalent manner: they felt interest and admiration for the blacks' reputation for intense sexuality and hipness. Their feelings contained some remnants of the civil rights fervor of the early 1960s and more than a dash of plain old American racism.

Although the blacks were less than accepted in an open way and were confused about their own status, they were certainly accepted at Sanctuary more than in the larger society. They kept returning, finding it possible to be somewhat comfortable in the loose and flexible atmosphere. They managed to create their own counter culture and did enjoy some sense of belonging and acceptance, even though an inconsistent one.

Black kids came, too, with all the conflicts which growing up in America had produced in them. The staff was confused about how to respond and what to do: counselors were especially concerned that Sanctuary, where nine-tenths of the staff was white, was not the best place for kids to work out these conflicts. Since qualified black personnel were more interested in working in all-black programs, it had been difficult to hire any to work at Sanctuary. The kids made it clear from the start that they expected the staff to be as racist as everyone else, and that it was up to the counselors to prove themselves. If there were in fact a better place for black kids to be, the counselors decided, they would undoubtedly find it; until then, Sanctuary was better than nothing.

Since most of the black kids had been excluded from significant white groups during the course of their lives, they were very slow to trust either staff or other kids, despite the numerous overtures made to them. Most of them preferred depending on their "brothers" and "sisters" for emotional support and confidences. Several kids spent most of their first few days at Sanctuary analyzing everything that was said for subtle racist content. Others chose not to hear the racial biases in the casual conversation all around them, concentrating instead on personal problems after apparently internalizing assumptions of failure and futility.

Friends

To convey a sense of how many black kids responded to the question of handling the predominantly white storefront, we will describe a small group that formed partially to protect and insulate itself from the pressures of whiteness and authority. John, Donna, Mike, and Sandy came to Sanctuary alone–Mike from New Orleans, Sandy from Chicago, John from Roxbury, Donna from New York. Within a few days, they were inseparable. Once together, they felt like a family and in control of the situation–almost indestructible. During the rare times any of them were alone, he or she was considerably more vulnerable. Although it sometimes seemed as if the group reinforced each individual's capacity for disruption, it was evident that the closeness and friendships were very important and beneficial to the kids.

John had grown up with an intimate knowledge of life on the streets and the techniques needed to survive there. He was the most practical and down-to-earth of the four. Assuming the role of volunteer in the hostel, he was very helpful in getting people lawyers and jobs. Especially involved in assisting his black brothers and sisters, he sometimes acted as a link between the staff and the black kids. When Donna got into legal trouble for petty larceny and then refused to show up in court, it was John who was able to get Donna to listen to a lawyer and go to court.

Mike and Sandy had hung around together all summer and were talking grandly about marriage plans, even though Sandy was only fifteen and Mike all of two years older. Both were very anxious about hurting the other and unsure of what they really desired and needed. After the entire group of black kids brought the situation to the staff, informal marriage counseling ensued. Although the black kids and the staff all tried to straighten out the situation and to be open and trusting, it was John again who finally brought about the open expression of feelings between Mike and Sandy and between the couple and the staff. Sandy and Mike finally decided to wait until she finished up high school. The settlement seemed to relieve everyone, and both the couple and the staff were excited by the fact that they had been able to talk to each other. Even though the kids had formed their (in some ways) exclusive group partially out of distrust of the staff, their having each other's support actually allowed them to relate to the staff and to the white kids at Sanctuary in a more positive and constructive way.

Danny

Many of the black males who came to Sanctuary had deep feelings of their own impotence in the world. A big, heavy guy with the beginnings of an Afro, Danny, age nineteen, came to Cambridge from Harlem where he had lived with his mother, an aunt and two sisters until the previous year. He managed to stay in school until the ninth grade when he began to have trouble with his hearing. Danny dropped out not long after that.

Arriving at the storefront three years later, his hearing problem had grown more serious because of a long-neglected ear infection. Danny had not gone to a doctor because he did not know how to find one or how to pay for one. A counselor escorted him to a clinic, where the infection was treated and Danny was fitted with a hearing aid. He was able to pay for it with an emergency grant from welfare, a provision which has, unfortunately, been dropped. The counselor stayed with Danny through the treatment at the clinic and the visit to the welfare office. Touched by the attention he was receiving, Danny told the counselor that this was the first time he could remember feeling anything but hostility and anxiety about spending time with a white person.

The counselor then worked on helping Danny, who was unskilled, inexperienced, and almost illiterate, to find a job. This was going to be no easy feat. They read the want ads together every day; at the same time the counselor casually helped Danny with his reading. After following a few leads with no results, Danny gave up the pretense of looking for a job and went on welfare. Although he had made the initial attempts, he never really seemed to think he would be able to get a job, or that he would be able to hold a job if he did get one. His lack of confidence was not surprising. Danny's mother, teachers, guidance counselors had expected nothing from him; they thought he would never amount to anything. Consequently he did not expect much either.

Danny's hopelessness was in part caused by the society's refusal to recognize black people in the educational system or in the labor market. Danny simply internalized other people's low expectations of him to the point that he believed himself inherently destined for failure. He was one of the people who blamed everything on himself, agreeing with the larger society that he was worthless and no good. Danny failed to recognize how much his plight indicted not himself, but society. The inability of young men like Danny to fit into any social institutions reinforced their sense of themselves as useless outsiders.

Marco

Feelings of impotence coupled with ambivalence towards authority were manifest in the case of Marco, a small but tough and wiry sixteen-year-old who came to Sanctuary shortly after it opened and then used the agency as home base for the rest of the summer. Black families often have their kids on their own at relatively early ages; police do not pick up many black runaways. Marco came in asking for help in finding a place to live and a job. Despite the three-night limit, he would often manage to sneak in after everyone else was asleep, when the counselor on duty had his back turned. In the morning there he would be, impossible to wake for breakfast, sometimes a recruit for morning clean-up. Counselors found job leads for Marco that he rarely followed up. Simultaneously appreciative and resentful of the staff's assistance, Marco wanted everything at the same time: to be able to be irresponsible and carefree but to have a stable roof over his head and maybe even some dinner.

Marco demanded a great amount of attention from other kids and from staff. One night, for example, he staggered into the hostel and managed to gasp that he had just heroically battled the cops—and then passed out. After attempting to revive him with smelling salts, a staff member took him to the city hospital emergency room. The doctor on duty there took one look at the limp body and said, "Oh no, it's Marco again!" Apparently Marco made regular appearances there; he would fake passing out and then rest on a stretcher until he felt like getting up.

Marco was very possessive of the storefront and the hostel as his home, despite his frequent conflicts with staff. He seemed very satisfied with the physical situation of living at Sanctuary, even if the staff did not think they were equipped to handle long term residence. One night early in August, while Marco was still trying to maintain that he had stayed at the hostel only two nights altogether and therefore was entitled to one night more, he had a real showdown with a staff member. Marco stood outside the hostel and yelled, so that all the neighbors and the people on the street could hear, that Sanctuary staff members were racist pigs, that they only threw out black kids, that his family had thrown him out too, and that no one ever cared about him. The counselor yelled back responses to some of his charges. Marco kept screaming. Suddenly both were out of breath. They looked at each other, grinned, and the counselor turned to go back into the hostel as Marco sped off down the street on a bicycle.

About three weeks after that incident, Marco was discovered smoking a joint in front of the hostel. When confronted, he said he did not know the no drugs rule, posted right over his head, where it had been since the hostel opened. Marco was flagrantly testing the staff, and the counselors told him that.

Not long after this incident, a counselor was explaining the three-day limit to a young girl who insisted that she would stay at the hostel until she wanted to leave even if she had to pretend to be very ill in order to do it. Marco interjected with a long discussion about how, when Sanctuary threw him out, he really got himself together. He lectured on how she should be self-sufficient and take care of herself, as he had learned to do. Marco was accepting our authority? No one could believe it was happening.

One evening near the end of the summer, Marco was just hanging around the storefront in a strangely quiet mood. Then he suddenly ran out into the traffic in what seemed to be a suicide attempt. The cars were going slowly enough so that they could stop for him. After being brought back inside, Marco had a long and really intense conversation with the counselor, in which he talked for the first time about missing his family and not having any kind of home. Marco never returned after that night.

Early in the fall a social worker from an established agency came in asking for Marco. It turned out that she had been in contact with him all summer and had been investigating halfway houses and vocational schools for him. She finally had the money to get him into a good program and wanted to find him so she could tell him the good news. The social worker called later to say that Marco had called her and that she had gotten him into a therapeutic commune and school. The existence of the social worker really surprised the staff, and made them reconsider their whole interaction with Marco. He had never mentioned her, though she was clearly in a better position to get him the things he needed: a saleable skill and a stable and warm residence where he could begin to work out his emotional needs with other suitable people. At Sanctuary Marco had tried to satisfy his need for parental and peer attention and emotional warmth, while he acted out his deep resentments against authority.

Marco wanted a home, which Sanctuary could not provide. Desperately needing constant attention, he became very possessive and frankly dependent. He was continuously testing the staff. By running into the traffic he was testing how much the counselors cared for him and was also manipulating them into showing their care by forcing them to retrieve him from the cars. In doing so, Marco was living out a familiar family cycle: asking for attention, wanting and not wanting parents, testing how much the parents cared, testing the parents' limits in setting and enforcing rules. The staff struggled to help Marco recognize, articulate, and hopefully work through his feelings of uselessness; the counselors fell into his game instead. They simply could not sustain a very deep relationship with him. When a staff person finally probed into his past, Marco split. In as real a sense as black South Africans are oppressed by their racist government, Marco was a victim of America's more subtle racism. Admittedly, unlike South African blacks, he was free to move and live outside of his black ghetto. But this freedom is illusory, since he has internalized the ghetto.

Harlan

Two black kids who came to Sanctuary were from the black middle class. Middle-class blacks have special problems: they are hit over the head with the fact that, despite their "solid" economic status, they will in all probability be unable to move beyond a certain point; middle-class blacks, furthermore, must deal with the hard-to-swallow fact that, even possessing the material trappings of the good life does not insure them recognition by white society. Speaking on a college campus, Malcolm X responded to a black intellectual's distant and disdainful remarks in the following manner: "Do you know what they call a Negro Ph.D. Professor?" Malcolm asked. "No," was the answer. "A nigger," Malcolm replied. These black kids were torn between their apparent nearness to white success, deceptively held out as being within their grasp, and their acknowledgment that they would always share the plight of other blacks.

Harlan was a black college student driven to try to succeed on white terms. He was short and thin, with well-groomed, medium length hair and a slight stutter. He spent the summer sleeping down by the river. When there was room, he squeezed between sweating bodies in the hostel, and then in the morning donned a uniform to go chauffeur a rich Boston lady; he was earning more money a week than a Sanctuary staff member received. Harlan was a sophomore at Stanford. Since he was also a California resident he had been able to get a special scholarship which paid tuition, room, and board, plus living expenses. Still, Harlan felt that he couldn't afford an apartment, that he needed his summer money to buy clothes to keep up socially with his classmates at school.

Harlan didn't talk much to other street kids. He only had contact with kids during the rare moments he would take out his harmonica and play the blues. He was incredibly good, and people responded. Even in the midst of his success and acceptance, however, he wasn't fully comfortable. He could only respond to another kid's honest admiration of his music with harsh self-criticism.

In a conversation, Harlan said he'd like to spend

more time on his music at school, but that he had to spend a tremendous amount of time on his regular coursework. He was a science major, not because he was particularly interested in sciences, he said ruefully, but because he might be able to get a good job in physics.

Harlan's loneliness made one want to cry. Here he was spending this degrading and uncomfortable summer, sleeping on the streets, being a chauffeur, to be able to live it up casually with his classmates in the fall. He seemed very isolated in the midst of the kids hanging around, and it seemed likely that he was not significantly more comfortable during the school year. He was a skinny black man trying to make it at Stanford, one of the symbolic citadels of the white man's world. He was unaccepted and uncomfortable everywhere. Life at Sanctuary offered some potentially easy personal encounters, just sitting around listening to a guitar and singing in the hostel, or helping the staff counsel runaways and bad-trippers at the storefront. There were other black kids around, usually friendly toward him, but he would not bring himself to talk to them either; he thought they were below him. The summer could have offered Harlan a three month respite from the kinds of pressures he bore at Stanford, but he was unable to unwind and let the facade down except for five minutes every three weeks when he played his harp. Even the flexible and open atmosphere at Sanctuary failed to break down the defensiveness Harlan had to maintain to survive in a world designed for whites.

Maybe it would have been too much for Harlan to let himself be vulnerable to any new set of people, no matter who they were, so he chose instead to isolate himself. Harlan was driving himself to work hard in situations where the odds were greatly against him (at Stanford), while he refused to try even a little in situations where success was more possible (at Sanctuary). He chose Stanford over a black college, or over a place where there were likely to be more blacks, physics over music, appearances at Stanford over relationships at Sanctuary—a continually self-defeating cycle.

Ace

Ace was another young black seriously confused about resolving his middle-class opportunities, his personal perceptions of the world, and the role he thought black people could or should aspire to. Ace felt that it was false for him to hang around pretending that he was a street kid, since he returned to his financially secure home each night. He was also made uncomfortable by his status as the child of one of the token black families in a Boston suburb. Rather than stay in suburbia much, Ace came into the Square, and dropped by Sanctuary frequently. Tall and broad, with a big Afro and a beard, Ace always wore work shirts and blue jeans.

Ace had graduated from a suburban high school that spring and seemed very bright and able when he chose to be. He hadn't decided what to do about going to college yet. He had built up a tentative rapport with a counselor named Ellen, and the two of them discussed this matter. He obviously had some feelings that he *should* go to college, so, with typical adolescent logic, all the arguments he offered were against college. He reminded himself that he believed school was pretty much of a drag, although he had been interested in his photography course. He was able to quote the statistics which show that black men with B.A. degrees earn about as much as white men with high school diplomas, and pointed out that according to simple arithmetic college would be a bad investment. Ellen pointed out the difficulty of trying to figure out not only how accurately one could estimate salary scales for ten years in the future, but also how valid it was to consider the rewards of meaningful work only in monetary terms. She felt silly trying to offer Ace the conventional platitude about college being the key to wisdom and did not say too much. She sensed that he was already deeply conflicted about the whole thing, and that finally he was the only one who could make a decision. She did tell him, however, that some staff people had been in college for varying amounts of time and had enjoyed it; she suggested people to ask about local schools. The counselor also threw in the suggestion that college might be a way to do more work in photography, although it wasn't the only way.

Ace said he hung around Sanctuary to get in on the action. Ellen, for one, had mixed feelings about his presence. She was definitely grateful for his being around one night when she was on duty alone and a big black guy started a fight and pulled a knife. When Ace arrived, he went right in to intervene and separated the two combatants; he then managed to convince the guy with the knife to get the weapon out of the building. The negative feelings stemmed from a kind of verbal interplay Ace and Ellen often had, apparently based on the tensions between black men and white women. Often he would talk not to her, but instead about her—she would notice how hot it was outside, and he would respond by saying that he liked the way she talked or looked. At one point, he only half-jokingly told her that she was the woman he wanted. She tried to hide behind her staff position and her five years' seniority, but it seemed a pretty weak defense. Other times, Ace would stand around and shower her with hostility.

Ace was interested in radical politics, especially the Panthers. Ellen gave him Bobby Seale's book *Seize the Time* after she had read it, and they talked about it at length. They had a very serious political discussion on the night Huey Newton got out of jail. Occasionally, however, he would withdraw from all the personal relationships he had with staff members and accuse them bitterly of not being as fair to black kids as they were to whites, of selectively enforcing the three-night limit on hostel stays on black kids and of calling down black kids for carrying weapons when they needed them for self-defense. He would threaten to expose Sanctuary's racism to the Boston Panthers, who, he promised, would wait only until the next dark night to come blow up the storefront. Counselors tried to argue with him that the charges were unfounded but as soon as they started to talk, he would walk out. A few days later Ace would show up with all the anger gone. One night there was an entry in the staff record book about Ace coming in and announcing to the general public how much he hated white people. The entry continued that race war was just narrowly avoided as Ace split before the white kids became involved in retaliation. When Ellen asked him later what he had meant by all that, he said he was just teasing, seeing what people would do.

Seething inside Ace were conflicts which he needed to be able to express, and his behavior was contradictory on many counts: for example, his desire was to try living on the streets, while at the same time he wanted to be able to go home. Ace was probably the most vocal about it, but the love-hate ambivalence he experienced toward white people represents feelings of many black kids who hung around in the storefront. Black nationalism is a very immediate and palpable identity. Many black kids refer to each other as sister or brother, and black students are demanding black teachers and black studies. It explains the frequent outbursts against whitey in general, and Sanctuary in particular. No matter how much Sanctuary was a groovy, accepting, warm place to hang out, it was still basically a white place, run by white people. It seemed as if most of the black kids were a trifle ashamed to be spending their time there: each disappeared periodically, and the time away allowed him to test his own resources and try to break any dependence which might have developed. All the blacks felt confused rather than totally hostile towards whites.

Ace was speaking for the other kids, too, when he accused Sanctuary of not being free from the subtle manifestations of racism which pervade not only liberal institutions but also larger society. Like Marco, Ace was continually testing. The staff response was that, although they were brought up in the same oppressive society and couldn't escape from absorbing some of its values, they were honestly trying to lead new lives with new values. Counselors could only promise that they took the problem of racism very seriously and were willing to try to struggle with each other when old, bad values came to the suface. The counselors knew it would be false to promise to be free from racism.

It was, moreover, very disconcerting for the staff to discover that black kids, who have every right to be angry, are indeed *very* angry. They carry knives more than white kids, and their emotional explosions are more frequent. Angry black kids can be very frightening. Although this observation was drawn out of the staff's own experience, they still felt awkward about it, knowing that the idea "blacks are frightening" is often used to justify repressive activities such as police brutality. Not wanting to fall back on black separatism as a reason to ignore black kids, as society does, they still were conscious of the limits inherent in the relationships they, as white staff members, could have with black kids. Was it just too confusing for counselors to act as role models? Could whites really understand the pressures blacks face? Had the counselors shared some of the important experiences which blacks have had?

The black adolescents who came to Sanctuary were accustomed to being harrassed by legal authorities (school officials, welfare workers, police); when confronted with *any* authority, they automatically put up defenses against their feelings of frustration and helplessness. Only too familiar with bad treatment from officials, black kids learn very young to meet antagonism with antagonism. Black kids' mistrust of white authority, based on repeated experiences of manipulation and harrassment, runs very deep and was maybe the single most serious obstacle to establishing a counseling relationship between a white staff person and a black kid. This defensiveness blocked the black kid who on some level would like to become involved with a counselor, but felt that she has to protect herself from the emotional damage she had come to expect out of dependent relationships with white people. Instead of direct communication, then, many of the black kids, like Ace, indicated their need for interpersonal relationships with counselors in indirect ways—by sexual advances, attention-getting activity, and hostile confrontations.

NOBODY'S CHILDREN

Kids on the streets are toughened by their experiences with state corrective institutions: courts, jails, and reform schools. (Mental hospitals also belong to this list, but they are discussed in the next chapter.) The intent of these institutions is to socialize according to specific standards. They stifle individuality and try to turn "criminals" into conformists. Too often these state agencies are ill-equipped to perform the rehabilitative functions that well-meaning but frightened legislators and communities expect of them. The care that kids receive from underpaid and sometimes callous staff is usually bureaucratic and impersonal; sometimes it is even physically brutal.

Most kids the staff sees are not successfully resocialized by reform schools. Even by the institutions' own admission, their rate of rehabilitation is very low. The kids, however, do not come out unscathed. They adapt to survive: they become cynical, manipulative, amoral. The staff found them very difficult to break through to at all. Angelo, Timmy, Maureen, James, and Ted are kids who had been through these institutions and then drifted into the street community, where their survival skills were practiced and taught to others. Unfortunately, Sanctuary can do little for the many graduates of the state penal system.

Angelo

Angelo never entered the storefront without a following of other kids. He was small and dark, with short but very thick black hair and deep, soulful brown eyes. He had the staff's attention within minutes after he first walked in. He said that he was diabetic, hadn't had his insulin in three days, and felt very near to going into a coma. He looked no older than sixteen, and he said that he was underage and a runaway. He talked a staff member (Phil) into calling up a doctor who had befriended him before; the doctor made special arrangements for Angelo to be seen by another doctor at a downtown Boston hospital. The counselor drove him to the hospital right away.

Angelo and Phil arrived back at the hostel an hour later with a supply of disposable syringes, enough insulin for a couple of days, and a prescription for more. Angelo sat on the platform, entertaining everyone with stories of his VIP treatment in the emergency room, and laughed with the irony of the dispossessed about having a prescription and no money to fill it. In a minute, someone was passing a hat, and panhandled quarters and dimes came out to pay for Angelo's insulin. A black kid, quietly sitting in the corner reading *The Autobiography of Malcolm X,* dropped in a dollar. Angelo pocketed the collection, turning to look at each contributor with an intense but quiet thanks. He left a little later with his arm around the waist of a tall, gentle girl named Sue, who lived in a commune in Cambridge which baked the bread for all the local organic food stores.

The next day, back with Sue, he had the whole

storefront's attention as he explained how he had run from a maximum security ward in the state hospital for the criminally insane. The note describing the incident in the staff record book read, "Angelo's stories about splitting from the hospital were fantastic, but something in the way he told them made you want to believe him—even me. Something inside me kept saying that the hospital he was talking about never had minors, but I forgot it as he talked. He had such details about the ward, and his escape plan was so complicated!" Angelo said that he wanted to break the story of the horrors of the hospital to the underground press; so a group of kids took him over to the office of one of the papers they hawked in the Square.

Angelo returned a little later. By now, he was walking with one arm around Sue and his other arm around her best friend, Anna. He came up to Erica, the counselor on duty, and interrupted her conversation with another kid to ask her to come into the office with him to talk about something very important. When he, Sue, and Anna were seated in the office, he told Erica that he had reported himself to the juvenile authorities. He referred to them as his "parents," perhaps trying to evoke her sympathy for his status as a ward of the state. He had scheduled a meeting with them for the next day, he said, and he felt he needed a lawyer there with him even though the meeting was an informal one. Erica agreed to try to get him a lawyer, but she reminded him it would be difficult because it was then Sunday night and the meeting was Monday. Erica wrote down her feelings about the interaction in the staff record book: "There's something not quite believable about Angelo. His quiet and earnest intensity is beginning to make me very nervous. I don't really think he could have been in that hospital, although he's obviously come from somewhere institutional. I guess that even if he didn't escape from the most famous one, all those reform schools are unbearable, and it does seem important for him to have a lawyer at that meeting. I wouldn't even have believed the meeting existed except that I had to call the juvenile authorities to get permission for Angelo to stay overnight at the hostel."

Erica finally located a lawyer. The lawyer asked to speak to Angelo, but Angelo said that he couldn't talk over the phone, that he'd rather the lawyer come to Sanctuary. The lawyer said that he was in Dorchester and that it would be inconvenient for him to come unless absolutely necessary. Angelo replied that it *was* necessary, and so the lawyer said he'd be down in an hour.

Angelo asked if he could use the office to talk personally to his friends about some things. Rich was working there, and he said that Angelo could come in if he didn't mind Rich's presence. Angelo then called Sue, Anna, and some other kids in to tell them why he had been locked up with the criminally insane. He told them how he'd first run away from home when he was eleven, for which he was put on probation. The state then sent him to reform school for stealing cars; he explained to those in the room that he *had* to steal cars since he didn't have love. He said that soon after he was sent to the maximum security ward of the state hospital for repeatedly running from reform school. He implied that during the car-stealing period he had also been a bikey, and Rich heard him mumble something about having killed someone in a gang fight.

Still working when the lawyer arrived, Rich listened to the second conference, where Angelo told a different story. He told the lawyer that this was his third runaway incident from a boy's industrial school and that the last time they said he would get an extra year's confinement if he ran away again. Angelo spent much more time talking about his family and his emotional problems. He said that his father, an alcoholic, had deserted the family, and that his mother had ten other children and a number of lovers, and thus had no time for him.

After the conference, the lawyer asked Rich to come

outside with him. He was furious, feeling that Angelo dragged him all the way to Cambridge to tell him some sob story to persuade him to confront the juvenile authorities on Angelo's behalf. Rich agreed that Angelo was being manipulative, but reminded the lawyer how bad the reform school was. Rich said that he felt it was right for Angelo to escape any way he could, even if it meant using Sanctuary and the lawyer in the process. Despite his anger, the lawyer agreed to go to the meeting and to call Sanctuary afterward to let the staff know what had happened. Rich wrote in the staff record book:

> I felt that I had to defend Angelo to the lawyer, knowing how easy it is for people who've never crossed the law personally to forget all they read and know about penal institutions. Knowing those conditions, it's hard to argue that anyone should stay there. Still, Angelo made me feel bad, too. It's hard to be in the position of knowing that a kid is trying to use you and will probably burn you and still go on trying to do the things that seem right for the kid's benefit. It blew my mind that Angelo kept looking at me innocently knowing that I'd heard both stories and refusing to acknowledge anything unusual.

In the meantime, Sue was confiding to Erica that she and Anna were both trying to have Angelo's babies. She said that the three of them planned to live in the woods and raise a family, grow vegetables and wheat, bake bread, tend sheep, and spin and weave. Erica swallowed hard and tried to talk to them about what they were getting into—the responsibility of having a child, how their plans would work, how far they could trust Angelo. Sue and Anna listened undaunted, but then were angry at Erica for doubting and questioning and not having faith in them. Erica's note in the record book:

> I did it all wrong. I should have asked Anna and Sue what *they* were feeling about the plan, talked

> about my fears of having children, tried to see if they could identify with them. It was so hard to try to question them about Angelo, whom I don't trust at all, without sounding patronizing and parental. I just panicked about Anna and Sue, who are really lovely and gentle and nice, being totally exploited by Angelo, and told them my doubts in a way that could only make them defensive.

The trio went off Monday morning to go downtown; they returned saying that all charges had been dropped and they were leaving that afternoon for Vermont to look for a farm. Sue and Anna were defiant; Angelo was exhilarated and grateful to us for getting the lawyer, who, Angelo said, had been really helpful. The three were still sitting in the storefront making plans with the other kids when the lawyer called to say that two warrants were out on Angelo, one for leaving reform school and one for stealing cars. Angelo had also been offered a deal of only two months more confinement which he had rejected. The lawyer commented wryly that Angelo had built a whole lot on getting out and that he obviously would lose face by going back. Rich called Angelo into the office alone, deciding not to humiliate him in front of Sue and Anna. He confronted him with his con game and his lies and expressed his own anger at being manipulated and used. Angelo sat there with his wide-eyed innocent stare, saying nothing. When Rich asked him what he was planning to do, Angelo said that he'd be able to figure that out, and he left the office quickly, almost before Rich was aware that he'd stood up. Angelo collected Sue and Anna and left.

Counselors heard later that day that Angelo, with Sue and Anna close behind, had wandered around the Common, panhandling and dealing his insulin syringes for money for what he was calling "the Cambridge Community in Vermont." His plan was to buy land that everyone on the Common could come live on. The trio promised that they'd leave directions at Sanctuary on how to get there.

The staff got a collect call from Angelo about three weeks later, which a volunteer accepted, thinking it was an emergency. Instead it was just Angelo, saying he was fine. He said he had been to the latest rock festival, was living in upstate New York, and would soon be married to a fine girl named Lillian. He asked for all his friends at Sanctuary and requested that a note be put up on the message board sending his regards. When we asked about Sue and Anna, he asked who we were talking about. He said he vaguely remembered them but that he had left Cambridge by himself. Checking later, Phil found that they were back at the bread-baking commune after a week's absence.

Phil and Rich laughed with tears in their eyes about that call and about Angelo. You could call him the great American con man, selling earnest love and communal country dreams instead of the Brooklyn Bridge. From a local social work agency Rich discovered that his family were ordinary Italian Catholics who lived in the South End and worked hard, but had more kids to feed than money to go around. They were strict about religion and confused about their son Angelo, who had been away from home since he was twelve. The boy had always been out of their control. We were confused about Angelo, too. It did not take the staff very long to see through his game, but they never did figure out what to do about it. Our staff could never reach him. The counselors were shaken, sensing the thickness of his defenses, the wall which protected him from the consequences of his actions. They were incapable of making even a dent.

Sanctuary's experience with Angelo raised many questions about dealing with kids who were trying to manipulate the staff. They permitted Angelo to have his own way and then became angry at him for hurting them. That is exactly the kind of cycle the staff should be able to avoid once they recognize it. Both kids and staff can fall into manipulating each other into acting out roles which are defined by past relationships. It seems very important to be continually aware that the staff may be used to fill gaps left by parents, and that the staff might use kids to play out their own fantasies about street heroes.

Counselors' tendencies to romanticize street kids as outlaws living outside conventional customs and morality suggests another problem: only a very thin line separates responses which are rightfully nonjudgmental and those which are voyeuristic. When a street kid comes in with a stolen camera, what is the proper response? To tell her to get it out of the storefront where it could get us in trouble? To join the other kids in asking for the story of where it came from, thereby lending some kind of tacit approval? To ignore it, again giving tacit approval? To show off our hip anticapitalism by distinguishing between stealing from a friend and stealing from a rich Harvard Square camera store? To come down hard on stealing in principle, neglecting the truth (as we see it) that excessive profit is stolen from workers and consumers anyway? To distinguish between stealing cameras, and stealing food or medicine which is necessary for survival? Counselors can beat the street kid at her own game by arguing that a camera is just a consumer product that belongs to the materialistic society which she rejects. They can show their concern for her welfare and tell her that she shouldn't steal cameras because she might get arrested, and that it's stupid to get arrested for stealing something she doesn't need. All of these *still* avoid a moral judgment. If morality is part of the society we want to build, however, it seems important to distinguish between moral and immoral acts. Although it is very difficult to do in a nonpatronizing or alienating way, the staff must talk about the values that they believe in, that are part of them and the lives they are trying to lead. Sanctuary's task is to learn how to talk about morality so that kids can respond openly. That is at least part of its counseling responsibility.

Timmy

It is not always easy to distinguish between what is revolutionary and what is criminal. Although we understand riots as expressing legitimate rage against oppressive conditions, that particular mode of expressing anger also involves the exhilaration of destruction. Timmy is a kid whose radical political ideas were treated by reform school authorities as delinquency. The staff didn't agree with them, but they were unable to help Timmy express his anger in constructive ways which would bring inner peace instead of anguish.

Timmy wandered into the hostel looking for a place to crash for a few days. He looked very young with his bright red hair and fair skin. Admitting that he was fifteen, he readily gave the staff permission to call his home so that he could stay at the hostel. The number he gave us to call collect turned out to be in Martha's Vineyard. A concerned woman answered the phone and said that it was fine for Timmy to stay with us. She asked if we would keep our eyes out for him and call her back any time we needed her.

Timmy spent the night and left the next day. He showed up again a couple of days later, doubled up in pain. Some kids he was with thought that he'd taken some acid with strychnine in it; they took him to the emergency room of the hospital. He received an antidote for the strychnine and a physical exam. The doctor said that Timmy looked exhausted, and also that he thought the boy might have tuberculosis. After the doctor took some tests, they all returned to the hostel. Timmy disappeared for the next few days. The tests finally showed that he had an acute infection. A counselor went looking for him on the Common and told him about the infection. He insisted that he was fine, and swaggered off. Later that night, he came to the hostel and admitted that he was very weak. He agreed to go to the hospital, and the next day the staff checked him into a good children's hospital.

During the next few weeks, the staff began to know Timmy better as they visited him frequently at the hospital, usually with one or two of his friends who would show up at the hostel a few minutes before visiting hours began. The counselors were impressed by his obvious intelligence and sensitivity and were excited by the flashes of warmth that would occasionally break through his distant and self-protective shell. We also found out a little about his background. His father was a career military man, very rigid and disciplined, and he told us that his mother was a writer. During the years from seven to thirteen, Timmy watched his father grow more cold and withdrawn, coming home less and less, and his mother spend fewer hours writing and more drinking. When he was thirteen, his father left on a volunteer mission to Vietnam. Not long after that, his mother was committed to a mental hospital. With no relative to take the boy, Timmy became a ward of the state.

When Timmy was twelve and thirteen, he spent a lot of time hanging around jazz places listening to music, and also frequenting art museums, sneaking in without paying and staying there all day instead of going to school. Since his state social worker was aware of his special interests and abilities, she tried to find an unusual placement for him. Timmy was uncomfortable with kids his own age—all his friends were older—so she fought to have this accepted by the bureaucracy. The authorities allowed him to settle in a commune of older people: two graduate students, a social worker, an architect, and a couple of law students. The commune did many things together; they went camping, did crafts, baked bread, and were very involved in antiwar work. Timmy spent his days at a free school in Cambridge, but came home every night for dinner. He was involved in all the house activities, including manning the phones at the antiwar committee's office and attending, though not participating in, the intense personal encounters which were part of house meetings. He really enjoyed the commune, but had a hard time opening himself up. People tried to be sensitive to his special needs and feelings, and he had close relationships with several individuals in the house. He was just beginning to really trust the group and open up when the school year ended. At that point the house broke up. Their lease had expired and their landlord refused to renew it, and most of the people had job plans in other cities. Timmy was on his own again.

His next placement was with a family connected to a university. The husband was a good man, but was much involved in his intellectual work and frequently distant. The mother was warm and interested in Timmy, but having neither children of her own nor much experience with kids, she found it difficult to distinguish between Timmy's need for freedom and his need for limits. She was unable to be much of an authority for him, and her husband failed by default, since he wasn't around very often. The situation was tense when again the school year ended and the couple made plans to go to their summer house on the Vineyard.

Timmy left with them, but was uncomfortable in the resort atmosphere. Even though there were other kids around, and he did like to sail, he missed his own friends, so he told the couple that he was going back to Cambridge. He said that he didn't want to mess around with spoiled rich kids, and that life in Cambridge was more real. They felt they couldn't stop him, they checked to see that he would be able to stay with friends and let him go. At that point, they apparently gave up on him emotionally. When the staff talked to them from time to time they seemed concerned and interested, but obviously were no longer letting themselves become too involved. They had been hurt by their failures with Timmy, and they felt rejected by his coldness. When Timmy returned to Cambridge, he and his friends spent their days on the Common. They started to experiment with different drugs and got reinvolved with Timmy's old political acquaintances, who were organizing people to go down to the Panther trial in New Haven.

When Timmy got out of the hospital, Sanctuary was able to place him and a friend in a camp program run by a group of people close to Sanctuary. The camp involved outdoor living and cooking, crafts, mountain climbing, and intense encounter groups. Timmy and his friend went there, but decided not to stay, preferring to structure their own time and to remain uninvolved with other kids. We tried to find the social worker who had spent so much time and thought on Timmy's placements and discovered that she had been fired. Timmy was arrested not long after that for handing out inflamatory political leaflets, but got off because of illegal arrest procedures. After that, Timmy became more extreme in all his undertakings. Having started doing junk, he got caught in the middle of a riot with a brick in his hand and a syringe in his pocket. He was placed in police custody, found guilty, and sent to boys' reform school. There he was proclaimed unmanageable and kept in a locked cottage with twenty-four-hour attendants.

All fall the staff was in contact with Timmy at reform school. His attendant described him as lazy and said he lay listlessly in bed instead of playing cards with the other inmates and was belligerent when not on drugs. He refused to read anything except prohibited political literature, to go to school, or to learn a trade. When counselors visited Timmy, he was sullen and removed. Sanctuary's relationship with him was worse than it had ever been.

It seemed obvious that Timmy was a sensitive boy

who had been battered by circumstances beyond his control—his father's coldness and decision to leave for Vietnam, his mother's breakdown, the commune's impermanence, the second family's inability to communicate with him. Timmy turned increasingly inward, marshalling the forces within him to survive on his own, independent of the adult world which had constantly failed to provide him with the emotional support and stability which he desperately needed. On his own, he was naturally drawn to the unstable world of the streets where drugs and independence are valued, and authority is regarded as malevolent. While drugs are used to dull the pain, mobility and toughness are the natural response to the jungle in which street kids perceive themselves. When Timmy tried to act politically, his efforts brought no tangible results. Manning the phones at an antiwar committee's office is a small but important act. But who in the radical movement has not suffered feelings of impotence as millions marched and thousands rioted, while Washington responded with the air war over Indochina? When Timmy exercised his constitutional right to free speech, all that saved him from incarceration was a cop's sloppiness in making out the arrest sheet and a judge who fortunately was concerned with procedural regularities. Finally, all the state can think to do with a politically and emotionally disaffected youth is to keep him locked up; his rate of rehabilitation is judged not by the quality of his ideas, but by his willingness to play cards. Timmy is not "lost." His sensitivity and emotional needs still exist—it is just a question of whether some person will be able, and will care enough, to reach him. At some future point, of course, it might become impossible.

Maureen

Like Timmy, Maureen was very bright and very tough. She was fourteen, tall and heavy, with long dark tangled hair and brown eyes. When the staff asked her to get parental permission to stay overnight in the hostel, she laughed harshly. She said that she was a ward of the state, that her parents had left her with her grandparents for a weekend when she was eight and that they'd never come back to get her. Her grandparents were too old to handle her, she said, and they'd tried to pawn her off on every institution in the state—orphanages, child guidance centers, state boarding schools, the home for little wanderers, foster homes. She tossed her head and said that she had refused to stay anywhere. A counselor called an agency she had mentioned; they said that she was telling the truth, so she stayed that night, and many more.

Maureen refused to allow herself to depend on Sanctuary. She came in and out, almost bristling even when simply asked how she was. She was continually hung up on some man or other, maintaining that the only person she'd let take care of her was a boyfriend. She was lonely and anxious; Maureen was not able to have good relationships with the men she chose; she was always planning to leave for the coast with one and then showing up a few days later saying they'd had a fight and refusing to answer any questions. Furthermore, she chose men who were as lonely and desperate as she was, not at all able to take care of her.

She came in one day shaking, thinking she might be pregnant and knowing that having a kid would end her mobility. Counselors took her to the free clinic to have a pregnancy test; it was negative, at which point she stiffened up again and stalked away. The only other time she showed any emotion occurred when a friend, with whom she sometimes stayed between boyfriends, had ripped off her sleeping bag. She came in crying, feeling really desperate and betrayed. A staff member found her a sleeping bag left in storage by a kid who had gone home suddenly. Maureen took it without a word, washed her face, and went outside again.

The agencies' records on Maureen described her as explosive and violent, unable to tolerate competition from other kids, or any kind of confinement by adults. The staff found that by the time she came to Sanctuary, the explosiveness and violence had been turned inward. She was superficially nice to other kids, but distant. Apparently convinced that no one could care for her, she chased men who obviously wouldn't, and ran the second anyone at Sanctuary showed any concern for her well-being. She was incredibly wound-up. Life on the streets allowed her to keep moving. The staff found no way to even slow her down, let alone talk her into resting a little.

James

James was nineteen; he had taken so much acid that his speech was hardly understandable. He was the youngest of eight children. His mother was old, sick, and worn out from taking care of eight children and a husband. The father was harsh; after he tried to sell insurance in Boston every day, he came home at night and usually commanded his family to wait on him. Joseph, the eldest, was a model child. He had done very well in parochial high school and won a football scholarship to Holy Cross. James, too, was well-behaved until he was sixteen. At that point, something in him cracked; we don't know why. He started taking lots of drugs, stopped going to school, learned how to steal VW's, and finally was sent to reform school for two years. When he came out, he found his old friends and started doing more drugs and stealing more cars. Older now, and having digested the tricks of the trade in reform school, he had learned not to be caught.

James came into Sanctuary in the middle of the summer. He was too spaced out to talk to the other kids; he occasionally could communicate that he needed a place to crash or dinner. Sometimes he would find someone as "out of it" as he was and they would excitedly toss ideas at each other. He ran his life by throwing the *I Ching*. He let it tell him when to steal VW's, when to take acid, which he sometimes did twice a week, sometimes not for ten days.

One staff member, Phil, pretty abstract himself, tried very hard to get in touch with James. They would sit for hours talking about mysticism, the *I Ching,* and Zen. In these conversations James would strain to be coherent and would sometimes succeed; but when James felt less "together," he would avoid Phil.

One day, Phil didn't show up for a meeting with James. James looked incredibly upset and began to cry as if he hadn't cried for years. Other staff people tried to talk to him and kept trying to find his friend, but all attempts failed. James suddenly picked up his *I Ching* and ran out the door. We never saw him again.

Sanctuary failed James. By one act of irresponsibility, one broken appointment, the counselor completely lost touch with a kid who had a lot of trouble making contact at all. It isn't clear where that relationship between Phil and James could have gone, but it meant a great deal to James. He seemed to be an intelligent kid, impulsive but sensitive. Finding no support at home, James created his own world, which proved to be quite confused and lonely.

James had two talents: stealing VW's and taking acid. The staff member who was closest to him felt that both preoccupations were games. VW-stealing was a high-risk game in which he constantly flirted with the possibility of being sent back to reform school. It represented a kind of dare. One night when James heard that a girl with hepatitis needed a ride to the hospital, he jumped up and said that he would be right back. He appeared later in front of the storefront in a fresh VW; before the staff knew what he was doing, he drove the girl away to the hospital. James seemed to take pride in having the nerve to steal cars. Car theft in this culture connects with ideas about masculine sexuality, self-sufficiency, and power, but James stole cars so often that it seemed that he might be strongly attracted to the idea of being forcibly returned to reform school, where none of those male ideals have an outlet. In sum, his counselor was left with the impression that James was still dependent on reform school–if not on the institutional life there, then on the prospect of being relieved of responsibility for his own life by being caught in a VW and returned to a cell.

James also seemed to resist taking responsibility for the pattern of his life in another way. His use of acid, supplemented by his own selective readings in Eastern religions, persuaded him that his entire life was predetermined. "Everything that happens has to happen; life is just a question of timing," he would say with apparent conviction. His counselor offered interpretations of *I Ching* hexagrams that honored the man who was conscious of numerous options and opportunities and chose a path among them. But James would insist that whatever path on which he found himself had been chosen: and he could make no other choice. James depended on this as a way of justifying the absurd risks that he was taking in stealing cars. These two games, VW's and acid, supported each other quite well, at least until James began to be impressed with his counselor's arguments about the *I Ching.* Even with Phil, James seemed to be disclaiming his own responsibility for his life; by developing a dependence on a counselor who would play the role of conscience, James could continue in his well-regulated cycles without having to answer to himself for what he was doing.

Ted

When Ted came in, he only wanted a place to stay. He was big for his sixteen years, but still awkward, with a broken-out face. This was his first successful escape trom reform school in Chicago, and although he knew the police were looking for him, he thought he would never be found in Cambridge. He'd been on the streets for about a month. He'd spoken to his mother from Ohio, but said she didn't care what he did. He was a ward of the state, anyway. He had a stomach ache from some bad acid, he thought, headaches, and maybe a fever, but he didn't want a doctor: just a place to crash. He met some kids who said he could go home with them, so he wandered out.

Every time Ted came back after that, he was tripping. Every time he tripped it was bad. He talked about being confused and depressed, and about plans of suicide. He mentioned fears about being a homosexual. Staff people talked to Ted about getting a lawyer to work on his legal status and getting a job, about taking hold of his life. He never really responded. He would just keep on mumbling that he was all alone and going to die.

We eventually discovered that all the agencies in the area knew him, and all felt equally hopeless. Ted drifted around, tripping and very sad. He said that he didn't want to talk, that we were all hassling him, trying to make him do things; all he wanted was to die. He disappeared for a while, and then a streetworker found him tripping on the Common. He stayed in the storefront until he was mostly down from the acid and then walked out the door. We never saw him again.

Reform schools did not help Angelo, Timmy, Maureen, James, or Ted. Sanctuary also proved incapable of helping these kids. The isolation they felt was too great, the defenses they built, too strong. Perhaps Sanctuary could have helped if it had had more time with them, or if the counselors had been able to get to the kids before their run-ins with the state's correctional system or institutions that are designed more to control than to rehabilitate.

Reform schools often try to rehabilitate by training kids for socially accepted and useful jobs. But these kids already view the jobs in question—and we would agree—as dead-end occupations. For the most part these are working-class kids who are being trained to stay in working-class jobs. Their parents, neighbors, and schools are working-class, and these kids have found the life surrounding them oppressive and intolerable. They want out, and society tells them there is no way out. And so these kids escape, both physically and emotionally. They run away; they take drugs; they engage in promiscuous sexual activity. They have only themselves to rely on, so at fifteen or sixteen they become tougher than middle-class people ever need to be.

Reform schools are just one step away from prison. The kids who are sent there are apt to be attracted not to the person who is gentle and sensitive, but to the toughest and most independent kid on the block, or in the reform school. The world in which they live is truly a jungle; rejected by parents, confronted by hostile authorities, these kids learn to be cunning and mobile. They have been hurt so many times by people professing to have their best interests at heart that they become distrustful and learn not to become vulnerable for fear of being shattered once again.

It is difficult for Sanctuary counselors to know what to do when they are confronted by such kids. The problem is larger than the interaction between one kid and one counselor. The staff tries to establish a bond of trust with these kids and to get them into more hospitable environments than either their family or reform school provides. But as Timmy's case shows, even this sometimes fails. The counselors never got close to Maureen or Angelo or Ted, and they lost their rapport with James.

NEEDED: A PLACE TO BE MAD

The Sanctuary staff views psychiatric problems not as symptoms of mental illness but as the signs of what might be called "difficulties in living." All those living on the streets are by society's definition, deviant, because they are not living at their parents' home (or, often, at any home), going to school, or earning a living. They are considered deviant because they have rejected the values of the dominant culture. Young people are, in fact, usually on the streets because they could no longer stand, or survive in, the social nexus of their homes, schools, jobs, or neighborhoods and amid the rules, roles, and expectations that are foisted upon them.

We do not believe that this class of people, simply because they are on the streets, is mentally ill. Whether or not a psychiatrist, however, would agree depends entirely on which psychiatrist is asked. If an action is to be described as a sympton of pathology, it depends not on the action per se, but on the values and norms of the person doing the evaluating. These kids may all be suffering from a collective ("sick") inability to deal with authority, and have all responded ("immaturely") by leaving the security of their homes for the hazards of the street. Yet it is just as possible that their leaving home might be a manifestation of the strength of their own will. Seeing that their home environments are unlivable, they move on even though their movement may have no clear—indeed may not have any—positive direction. A similar disagreement persists concerning the mental health of radical political activists.

Deviants all, it makes sense that street people would reject society's definition about who is normal. Not only do they refuse to ostracize, they even support individuals who display behavior apparently caused by marked emotional conflicts. Despite their odd manners, bad judgment, the great emotional demands they make on others, and the annoyance and trouble they cause, many kids succeed on the streets to a greater degree than would have been possible in their home environments, which demanded more conformity, obedience, and less trouble. On the street, a great deal of tolerance and comfort is given to individuals whom society labels neurotic or psychotic. Currently, these terms are used largely as tools to categorize and control people. In general, it seems as if these labels are used to cover the often unavoidable conflicts which occur among people, to obscure the real conflict or problem the individual is facing. In the more specific case of street people, officials often use these terms as aids to incarcerating troublesome people, and also to avoid consideration of the conditions which caused the young people to have such torturous conflicts.

What society calls mental illness is the individual's own way of working out the problems and conflicts she encounters in living. Rather than judging such actions as running away or living on the streets as neurotic or psychotic, the Sanctuary sees people who act in such deviant ways as trying to do exactly what they are capable of doing under the given circumstances. Considering the difficulties, dangers, and unpleasantness involved in living on the streets, many young people would not be attracted to it if they had any real and viable choice in the matter: street kids often have nothing left. For this reason alone, counselors work as hard as they can to encourage young people to work at their lives so that they will be able to survive, even if on the streets.

For many street kids, struggle is familiar. Half the young people who came to Sanctuary during the summer originated in poor, working-class homes, and this percentage grew sharply during the fall and winter. The objective conditions caused by living in poverty create a whole spectrum of difficulties in living. Spiro Agnew is correct in saying that "if you've seen one slum, you've seen them all" in that poverty is, simply, poverty and has common distressing effects on people. His statement is outrageous because it reveals his indifference to the American pattern of tolerating stultifying poverty in the midst of enormous wealth. Admittedly, the feeling of not having enough money causes anxiety wherever it occurs. But the effects of worrying about keeping up with the Joneses are inconsequential compared to the strain of constantly struggling to feed your family and keep it together, to pay the rent, to buy medicine and a doctor's care—struggling, in short, to survive.

Angered by the blatant injustice of their parents' hardships, young people cannot bear the thought of struggling in as poor an environment as their elders have, despite the love they feel for their parents. When men and women get nowhere, no matter how hard they work, they grow bitter and hopeless. In light of the problems caused by the vastly unequal distribution of wealth in America, it is understandable that many of Sanctuary's young people come from homes that are tortured, broken, or somehow mangled. The high incidence of alcoholism, desertions, incest, and violence in the homes of the poorer kids who come to Sanctuary is no less than astounding. A social worker assured us that these patterns are "quite common" yet his words were cold comfort; these phenomena are not so much unavoidable elements of the human condition as tragedies of a systematically neglected and exploited class of people, the poor.

One theory about the definition of the most prevalent modern madness, schizophrenia, states that all people have a certain capacity for this illness; the capacity is a function of two factors: the healthiness of the person's early environment and relations with his parents, and the intensity of the life crises he will have to face. Since poor people have the most severe "difficulties in living," it is logical that they suffer a disproportionately large share of mental illness. This fact is damning to the society which perpetuates the poverty, whether it does so because it needs cheap labor or through benign neglect. Madness does not just appear. As R. D. Laing states in *The Politics of Experience,* "It seems to us *without exception* the experience and behavior that gets labeled schizophrenic is a *special strategy that a person invents in order to live in an unlivable situation* (pp. 117-118)." Mental illness among the poor is not merely a result of "poor adjustment." How do you adjust to rats in the kitchen and no way out, anyway? Or to personal family problems that reflect society-caused pressures and are also responses to the objective conditions of poverty? The economic and political system which maintains a class of habitually poorly fed and downtrodden people must bear some blame for the ruined lives and burned-out stares visible wandering through the wards of state mental hospitals.

In this chapter we will attempt to discuss further difficulties in living occurring in the lives of the street people who came to Sanctuary to illustrate the ravages which mental hospitals sometimes inflict on young people and the staff's conflicts about sending individuals to asylums, to examine the street scene's toleration of what society labels as deviance, and to put forth some ideas about new places of treatment. Of the four men and three women discussed here, all but two—a male high school teacher and a young woman who worked as a clerk—come from poverty-line backgrounds. Three of the individuals discussed had been in mental hospitals for varying lengths of time before they came to Sanctuary; by the fall five had either returned or been committed to hospitals.

MADNESS AND THE FAMILY

Sanctuary's counselors often perceived the parents of young people who came for aid to be unconsciously perplexing and harming their children by speaking and behaving in ways which Laing has defined as "mystifying." Laing states: "To mystify . . . induces confusion in the sense that there is failure to see what is 'really' being experienced, or being done, or going on . . . This entails . . . the substitution of false issues for the actual issues" (p. 344). In this same article, entitled "Mystification, Confusion, and Conflict" (in Ivan Bozoermenyi-Nagy and James Framo, eds., *Extensive Family Therapy),* he continues "Mystification is particularly patent when . . . one person appears to have the right to determine the experience of another or complementarily, when one person is under an obligation to the other(s) to experience, or not to experience, himself, them, his world, or any aspect of it, in a particular way (p. 348)." When parents' words or actions seem to contradict each other, to deny what the youth experiences as actually happening, to negate an aspect of the youth's very being, then the parents are setting the scene for the madness of their children. These parents love their children no less than other parents, but for various reasons, often to maintain a balance in the way they perceive themselves or their children, they unwittingly offer their children frustratingly inconsistent pictures of reality. In the cases of Susie Sargent, age twenty-two, and Rose Fuller, age fifteen, we believe that the parents "mystified" their daughters in ways which were as damaging as they were obvious.

Susie

When Susie walked into the hostel last summer, it would have been very difficult to tell that the attractive, red-haired, thin, and pale young woman was experiencing serious emotional conflict, or that in three weeks she would be in a mental hospital. During the first days that she hung around, however, her counselor Erica realized that Susie was extremely nervous and flighty: she could not focus on any question for more than a few minutes. Susie could not remain calm despite the many tranquilizers she gulped down. Confiding in Erica, Susie said that she had worked as a clerk and lived with her parents in Lincoln until about a month before. At that time she got into a fight with her father, who beat her up, although she was reluctant to discuss why they fought.

Finally she explained that, although her parents said she was free to come and go as she liked, they controlled all her dealings with men to the point that she had to date on the sly. "Once when I came home for a date at just ten minutes after midnight," she complained to Erica, "my parents told me that I was 'no good' and then wouldn't say a word to me for days." Susie stated that she had been seeing a psychiatrist during the previous year; she added that he had given her the tranquilizers but that she had not seen him since she left home. Asked if her parents knew whether she was still alive, Susie responded that she did not care about them, but soon after called them to say that she was safe at Sanctuary. In general, Erica tried to impress upon Susie that if she really meant to live on her own, she better start planning where she would go and how she would earn a living.

After a week in the hostel, Susie "flipped" over a well-known hippie named Buffalo Bob, whom she met one afternoon on the Cambridge Common. She spent most of the day and night with him, but around three o'clock that morning she returned to the hostel in tears because she and Bob had quarrelled. The next morning Erica found Susie much more unstable than she had been two days before. At this time Susie was wearing an ill-fitting polo shirt and a pair of shorts that obviously had belonged to someone much larger than Susie. Erica tried to talk, but the girl was simply too upset. Around 10 a.m. Bob "dropped by" for Susie. The pair had a quick reconciliation, Susie casually said goodbye to Erica, and the couple left.

During Susie's absence, Erica received two phone calls from Susie's parents asking the whereabouts of their daughter. Since Susie was legally an adult, Erica told them she was not obligated to give out any information and that all she knew was that Susie had been physically well the last time she had been in the hostel and had been relatively happy. The father became quite angry, saying that he had already spoken to one of the "kids" (who did answer the phone sometimes) and knew that his daughter had gone off with "some drug-taker" and was running around "half-dressed with her behind showing." He shouted that his daughter was completely innocent sexually and that he would hold Sanctuary responsible if she got "in trouble," by which he meant pregnant.

Three nights after she left, Susie called from a suburb to say that Bob had split for an hour that morning and had not returned, and that she was unable to get herself back to Sanctuary. Her voice conveyed a sense of sharp pain which prompted the counselor who answered the phone to drive out and collect her immediately. Susie kept repeating that she loved Bob, that he really wanted to marry her, and that she was now bearing his child. It became clear that she had slept very little since she had met Bob four days before; she talked compulsively every minute, needing to make people listen to her. She was terrified of being alone.

Out of desperation she called her old psychiatrist, who mentioned that her parents had called and that they were concerned about the kind of people Susie had been spending time with. Later she learned that her parents had also called the hostel several times, insistently trying to find out where she was. Furious at her parents' intervention, she called them to tell them to stop "spying" on her. They denied that they had called anyone concerning her, saying that she should be less "self-centered" and have "more trust" in her parents. These interchanges further upset Susie.

At Erica's suggestion, she went to the free clinic to see a therapist, who comforted her a little, and who explained that although she might be pregnant, she could not be pregnant by Bob. After all the events of the week, Susie could clearly not take any more. She walked around the hostel for a few hours telling everyone that she was a "tramp," that she had not deserved Bob because she was already pregnant, and that he had been right to leave her. Left alone for an hour that night, Susie lightly cut herself several times with a scissor she found.

Erica then believed that she could no longer insure Susie's safety, and decided to call her parents, who could afford a private mental hospital, to come pick up their daughter. By this time Susie herself began to feel that she was "going mad," and she was frightened of what she might do. When Erica called the girl's father, he was polite and concerned and said that he would come for Susie in an hour. But two hours later he had not arrived yet, and so Erica called again. This time Mr. Sargent said he had decided against coming because he did not believe that Susie really needed help or that she had called her psychiatrist because if either were true, he insisted, the psychiatrist would definitely have called him. Susie begged to speak to him and blurted out, "I'm going to have a baby." Mr. Sargent responded with "That's impossible. Stop acting. If you want to, come home, but I'm not going to pick you up." Erica took Susie to the city hospital for an overnight psychiatric evaluation. The next morning, after urging by the psychiatric staff of the hospital, the Sargents came to take her to a private mental hospital.

Although being abandoned by Bob triggered off Susie's episode of "madness," she was anxious when she began the relationship, even though her counselor did not fully realize this when she arrived. By refusing to admit to calling the psychiatrist or Sanctuary, Susie's parents acted in a mystifying manner by substituting a lie for what their daughter knew to be true and damaged her ability to trust them. Susie felt that the calls represented her parents' intention of continuing to control her life and their refusal to consider her leaving home a meaningful break. These feelings understandably called forth Susie's deep reaction against her parents; it was their intention to control Susie that her parents sought to deny by refusing to admit the phone calls and feigning indifference to the whole subject of their daughter. Instead, they invoked the false issue of Susie's alleged lack of trust in them.

When Mr. Sargent explained why he wasn't coming to get Susie, he mystified the situation by denying her strongly felt experience of madness, insisting that Susie was merely acting, trying to manipulate him. Mr. Sargent was saying, in effect, that he would decide what Susie was experiencing, just as he decided on the other areas of her life. Beneath his refusal to help Susie might have been some desire to punish her for having left home. If Mr. Sargent tried to deny that Susie was really sick or in trouble, then he reduced his guilt at possibly harming her by contributing to her leaving home. Susie's home was mystifying in that she was told she was free, despite her own accurate perceptions that her parents were determined that things remain otherwise. By curtailing her freedom to date, Mr. Sargent used the false issue of obedience to mask the real issue, his attempt to deny Susie's desires for relationships with men. When Mr. Sargent told his daughter that it was "impossible" that she was pregnant, he meant it literally: no matter what she thought or how many men she had slept with, he had decided that she was a virgin and therefore could not be pregnant.

Rose

Rose Fuller, a black girl from Roxbury, called the Sanctuary "hotline" up to five times a day during the summer. In a shrill, high voice she gave a number of names to the different counselors who received her calls; it took at least a week for the staff to figure out her real name and that she came from Roxbury, not Newton. She spent most of her time cooped up in her mother's hot, tenement apartment. A widow for many years, Mrs. Fuller only allowed the girl out when she herself could accompany her; when Mrs. Fuller's friends came to visit, she often locked the girl up in her room. Calling Sanctuary was Rose's only escape from her hell of isolation, and counselors spent more than a hundred hours on the phone with her.

The counselors considered Rose to be painfully lonely, intelligent, sexually frustrated, and confused about separating her fantasies from reality. Rose's conversations showed that she had had no experience in dealing with real people in real situations; all she had were her fantasies. Right after saying that she wanted to become a lawyer, she would become terrified because she thought she was occupied by a "devil." Rose complained that her mother picked all her clothes for her and refused to allow her to wear a bra. The girl would become involved with male counselors in a desperate plea for sexual recognition: while asking the staff members to love her, she struck out at them with a string of obscenities. About the time the staff began to discuss whether it would do any good to try to convince Rose to see a therapist, Mrs. Fuller called with a request and some information. After stating that Rose had been in mental hospitals for a number of short stays over the previous years, Mrs. Fuller asked the counselor to try to convince Rose to take the (quite strong) tranquilizers which her current psychiatrist had prescribed, but which she had steadfastly refused to swallow.

A few days later a counselor learned that Mrs. Fuller had succeeded in making Rose take the medication by promising that the girl could spend the next month, August, visiting with an aunt and cousins in Chicago. As August approached, the mother announced that she did not have the money to send the girl on vacation. So Rose sat at home, trapped by her domineering mother, her own confusion, and her voluminous fantasies. She was very depressed. Later that week, when her mother was out, she called Sanctuary to announce that she had taken "thirty little white pills." While the surprised counselor asked her why she had done it, she excused herself "to take some more," put down the phone and then returned. Although the counselor suspected that the call might simply be a ruse to attract attention, he knew about her recent depression and felt he could not take the chance of leaving the girl alone.

He and a volunteer arrived at Rose's apartment shortly after the girl had told her mother, who had just come home, that she had taken "thirty-five pills" and was "going to die." All three people helped carry the now quite ill girl to the car; the process attracted a small group of onlookers, one of whom called out quite loudly, "the crazy girl is sick." On the way to the hospital, Rose complained bitterly of the rudeness of "those terrible people" who had stared at her. Mrs. Fuller countered this by reprimanding Rose for saying "bad things" about the neighbors, who, the mother said, were in fact not even watching her, and who really liked her. The transparent falseness of the statement puzzled the counselor and did not seem to convince Rose, although it did quiet her on the subject. Rose's stomach was pumped, and the pills turned out to be aspirin. Her mother took her home later that night.

After this incident the mother evidently began to trust Sanctuary a little and called a counselor to ask if she might bring Rose in for an afternoon. The counselor said that would be fine, and added that he always had wondered why Rose had not come before. The mother answered that previously the girl had never wanted to go. When the counselor asked Rose what had changed her mind about visiting, she replied that, weeks before, she had asked her mother if she might come but had been refused until that morning when her mother told her that she was taking her to Sanctuary "whether she liked it or not." During the few times that Rose was brought to the hostel, she seemed to enjoy it. She seemed very tense, however, and often tried to attract the attention of the boys hanging around, alternately calling to them and insulting them. Physically developed for her age, she looked strange dressed in loose-fitting clothing really suitable for a much younger girl. Rose continued to call Sanctuary through August.

Four times over the summer counselors became excited and enthusiastic because they had managed to have a long, seemingly rational and hopeful talk with Rose. The girl would speak of attending secretarial school, getting a job, working more with her therapist. Within two days, however, her counselor would find her back in her "crazy" state, inhabiting an unreal world, talking desperately to affirm the fact that she really existed, even confessing a murder which she had fantasized. By summer's end, the staff decided that they should not continue their relationship with Rose since they felt that they were making no headway with her and that she was also taking up far too much staff time. A female volunteer then decided that she wanted to work with Rose on an on-going basis, and the case was turned over to her. After a few months, the volunteer arranged to have Rose admitted to a private mental hospital and continued to do work with her.

When Mrs. Fuller held out the vacation to make Rose take her medicine, she was clearly tricking her daughter into doing what she herself wanted, pretending that in the future she would give Rose what Rose wanted. Even though Mrs. Fuller lied for what she might have construed as Rose's well-being, the act constituted yet another blow in the series that was destroying Rose's capacity to trust her mother. Although Rose was still a teenager, Mrs. Fuller made up almost all the girl's world, all that Rose could test her own reality and being against. About Rose's not coming to Sanctuary, Mrs. Fuller acted and spoke as if the idea originated in the girl's mind, instead of her own. The mother behaved as if the decision were up to the girl, when, in fact, she had complete power in this as in all other matters concerning Rose. The mother was in effect subverting the girl's will by retaining real control and by making it seem that the girl was responsible.

Similarly, when the girl saw the neighbors staring, her mother mystified the situation by forbidding her to see it in this way, although the girl's perception of the situation, as the counselor corroborated, was quite correct. This action could only result in making Rose doubt her own mind, disregard what she saw and experienced in favor of what her mother stated "actually" happened, what Rose "should" have seen. Finally, concerning Rose's maturity, Mrs. Fuller again denied that Rose could feel and see, that she was, at least physically, a fully-developed woman. By refusing to allow Rose to dress in ways suitable for her age, Mrs. Fuller could deny that the girl was, in some ways, already a woman, that Rose would have sexual feelings, that she might eventually leave her. Just as Mrs. Fuller was the world to her daughter, so Rose was all the mother had had since the death of her husband. Mrs. Fuller's denial of Rose's sexuality mystified the girl by severely complicating the inherently difficult task of a fifteen-year-old's becoming secure in her own sexual and personal identity. Since Rose was not recognized as a sexual being, she probably experienced her own sexual feelings as evil (the devil who occupied her?), or at least as something to be hidden from her always-present mother. Rose's isolation, furthermore, could not possibly aid her need to work out her feelings about being a woman and her feelings toward men—a need demonstrated by her appealing to and at the same time cursing both the male counselors and the boys in the storefront. Although the counselors had relatively brief contact with Mrs. Fuller, they could see how she was mystifying Rose and thereby threatening the girl's sanity.

MENTAL HOSPITALS

When it becomes necessary to send a young person to a mental hospital, the counselors believe that in some ways they have failed, because they could do nothing more creative than cart the individual off to an institution in which the counselors themselves have little faith. Mental hospitals certainly do prevent socalled crazy people from endangering others or creating a nuisance for socalled normal people, and they provide physical safety and rest for the patient/inmate (although psychic harm is another matter). They rarely cure anyone, however, or make them better able to live up to their potential. From Sanctuary's experience with these institutions, it is clear that they are useful as locations which permit people to be "mad," perhaps to act in asocial, impolite, even obscene ways without fear of social or legal punishment.

At most public hospitals, patients receive little therapy and enormous dosages of drugs, which are used at least as much for "patient management" as for helping people. It is standard procedure for a patient to be assigned a social worker already overburdened with cases; if she's lucky, the patient may talk to a doctor once a week. Some patients only see a doctor when a decision must be made about their case. Otherwise, they spend time on the wards, watching television, milling up and down bleak corridors and sometimes around the hospital grounds, constantly under the watch of attendants. At most private hospitals, the atmosphere is somewhat less dehumanizing and all the proper services are available: many patients see a doctor once a day; recreational facilities are open. On a deeper level, however, the records of both kinds of hospitals at helping people are so low that one doubts the validity of their claim to be hospitals, that is, therapeutic facilities at all. We do not mean that the people who work long and hard in mental hospitals are doing anything but their best; serious problems, however, do exist with the management of mental illness in America.

Most Sanctuary kids are committed to public mental hospitals, which legally, as Erving Goffman states in his book *Ayslums*, have primarily a custodial function: "If we view the mentally ill as persons that others have a certain kind of trouble with, then the custodial role of the hospital . . . is justified; the point, however, is that service to the patient's kin or neighbor . . . is not necessarily a service, especially not a medical service, to the inmate (p. 353)." This viewpoint is crucial for understanding how street kids or other young people in many cases accurately perceive being sent to mental hospitals: not as a cure, but as a punishment for being too socially troublesome.

Most young people do not commit themselves to mental hospitals but are instead involuntarily hospitalized by parents, relatives, police, and so forth. Imprisonment only adds to the hostility and alienation which probably were part of the reason they were committed in the first place. Young people are further scarred by the empty, cold, distasteful life they find within hospitals. Thus, another oppressive institution is added to the already long list of groups, such as families and schools, which have failed or betrayed them. By systematically stripping a new patient of most of her belongings, ignoring her whenever possible, and controlling every aspect of her life, hospitals can be highly destructive of a person's sense of self, especially for the young who are struggling to develop an identity. Furthermore, the hospital staff accepts the presence of an individual in a mental hospital as proof that the person is indeed "mad," and all her actions, inactions, protests, and even warm feelings are interpreted from this point of view.

Just as the criminalization process has a very real and costly effect on all the kids who run afoul of the law, hearing from all sides that all one's actions are "insane," or that one is not really responsible for anything one does, since one is crazy, irreparably damages a young person's conception of herself. Finally, most working-class youths committed to mental hospitals suffer a great deal simply because they have not learned to behave and respond in the obedient, middle-class manner that will serve them best in mental hospitals as well as in all other American institutions. Adolescents are fiercely uncompromising, and they cannot overlook the fact that they feel and are treated more like prisoners than patients. They perceive the psychiatrist to be first a judge, and then a doctor. Of course, hospital staff dismiss all complaints about the hospital as symptoms of the patient's madness.

Harry

The case of Harry Burns illustrates the brutal and debilitating effects imprisonment in mental hospitals can have on adolescents. When Harry came to Sanctuary, he felt very depressed and desperately lonely. He was a tall, thin, still-awkward nineteen-year-old who wore his hair cut short. Soon after Harry arrived in early July, he attempted to place a collect call to relatives he had in Maine; for some reason, they refused to accept the charges, which made Harry very angry. About a week later, he became infatuated with a pretty but freedom-minded girl who stayed with him for two days and then moved on to another part of the city. Both these rejections intensified his usual fears that he was unloveable and that no one cared about him. He complained about this state of affairs bitterly to everyone who would listen.

Harry spent some time with Randy, a counselor, whom he talked to whenever he could, and, in a subtle manner, followed around a good deal. Randy discovered that Harry had spent two years in a state mental hospital and that he had finally been able to leave on his eighteenth birthday. Harry remarked that he had become addicted to barbiturates during his stay in the hospital, and that it had taken him several months to get off "downs." His father, with whom he had never gotten along, had committed him. With some bitterness, Harry told Randy what he hated most about the mental hospital: "I can't remember anyone ever saying a word to me." His mother had visited him only a handful of times during his commitment; although he occasionally wrote to her now, he never went home for fear of an explosion with his father. Harry's story of his two-year stay in a mental hospital was corroborated by a local health clinic where he was well known.

A few weeks later, at a crash pad where Harry was spending the night, a girl almost died from a heroin overdose. Partly due to his own narrow escape from "downs," this upset Harry greatly. The next day at the Sanctuary hostel, he kicked in the door of the men's bathroom when he suspected that someone was shooting up inside, although there was only a boy washing. The counselor on duty informed Harry that he expected him to help pay the cost of repairing the door. We don't think that Harry did anything clearly wrong. Considering that people are far more important than property, breaking down a door is not a grave offense if the action can help someone.

When Harry visited Randy later that night the counselor tried to make him think about how he was going to support himself. Randy was eager to have Harry get settled, since he believed that this would make the youth feel more secure. Although Harry had been in Cambridge for more than a month, he had begun neither to consider how he would support himself nor to think about what he wanted to do with his life. Harry not only lacked motivation to work, but also did not know how to begin to get a job. When Randy found him a part-time opening, Harry did go to work but left within two hours because the foreman yelled too much.

Randy had not heard from Harry for a month when he called, very angry, to complain that he was not being treated fairly in a Boston health clinic. Randy checked it out and found that the clinic was very crowded and simply could not take Harry when he thought it should have been his turn. The counselor discovered that Harry had exploded at the receptionist, and a doctor had come out and gotten angry right back, telling Harry that he needed a mental hospital rather than a health clinic. Harry called Sanctuary throughout the fall, sometimes to request a thermometer, sometimes just to say hello. The counselor also received phone calls from nurses in several hospitals around Boston, who usually said that Harry was a patient of theirs, and that he had wanted Sanctuary to know where he was.

Harry was constantly getting into minor troubles: in addition to breaking the door down and the scene in the clinic, he had been arrested several times over the summer for loitering. He was preoccupied with himself, believing that he had an entire flock of ailments; he sought treatment continuously. Randy could only conclude that the youth's affinity for trouble and his medical melodrama were but half-concealed demands for sorely needed attention. The counselor realized, however, that in breaking down the door, Harry was trying to live up to the values of Sanctuary by helping others and, on the same level, to please the counselors, even though in a self-dramatizing way.

Possibly a result of his years in the mental hospital, Harry was socially helpless and incompetent, unable to relate to people except in a dependent capacity, as if he were a young child. Although he had managed to kick his addiction to barbiturates, he was still addicted to hospitals and agencies, as his behavior demonstrated. A hospital automatically gives attention to sick people and could provide a place for Harry to be both dependent and, quite literally, regularly attended. Without a big change, Randy could not imagine him living independently instead of hovering around service agencies, begging for institutional love.

To repeat, Laing says "behavior that gets labeled schizophrenic is a special strategy that a person invents in order to live in an unliveable situation (*The Politics of Experience,* p. 115)." Goffman explains that the desolate life of a mental hospital patient may, in fact, become untenable if the patient does not play along with the institutional line: since she is a patient, she must be insane. In this case, for Harry to rebel against this judgment, to maintain his belief in his own autonomy, he also would have had consciously to consider his father's committing him in no less than a treacherous light; Harry would have had to think of his father as simply "evil."

It seems reasonable that Harry, sixteen when he was committed, internalized his environment's view of himself and adopted the negative identity of madness. Since he had been continually inculcated with the fact that he was incapable of living on his own, of doing anything in a sane manner, why should he now be able to feel that he was capable of living a meaningful life without the aid of a protective institution? Committed for two years, Harry had become, and might continue to be, a dependent mental patient for life.

Faced with a young person who is disfunctioning in a wild manner or who does not respond to any attempt at communication, the counselor must make a torturous decision. On the one hand, she is tempted to decide that she cannot handle the case, that the person needs more help and care than she can give. She thus turns to a psychiatric evaluation, which may lead to committing the patient to a mental hospital and all the dangers which accompany this step. The counselor may feel that, given the physical set-up of the counseling service, she will not be able to insure the supervision needed to prevent the young person from injuring herself or others or simply wandering away, which would probably get the young person into further trouble. In contrast, if the counselor tries to handle the case without resorting to mental institutions, she might do so because she believes that the young person needs a trusting relationship more than "treatment," or that the person would not get needed treatment at a mental hospital anyway. Whatever she does, uneasiness will result, since it is always possible that in any particular case psychiatric care would have made the difference, although it is rare that the hospital environment can help much.

Bill

Because of these real dangers, the decision to commit Bill Andrews, a tall, well-built, handsome nineteen-year-old from Stoneham, sharply divided the staff. His father, a truck driver, had died three years before; he had dropped out of school shortly after that time, and during the previous year had taken several hundred acid trips. Bill hung around the storefront regularly for about five weeks.

Although Bill liked the other kids in the storefront, he did not talk much except to people whom he felt he really knew. He talked very slowly, often forgetting what he was in the middle of saying, and he had a great deal of trouble with the minutiae of life, such as his shoelaces. Even by the relatively loose definitions of the Cambridge street scene, he was a very spaced-out young man. Eventually he became friends with a volunteer named Ed.

When Ed asked why he had dropped out, Bill explained that he had liked school well enough, especially reading stories, but he could not see the point of learning the other subjects since he knew he would never go to college. When Ed, a typical middle-class Harvard student asked Bill why he had thought college was out of the question, the youth explained that very few students from his school ever went on to college. Bill told Ed that he had started tripping on weekends when he was fifteen because there was nothing else he wanted to do and because he became very close to his friends when they all dropped acid together. The next year, just before he left school, he said that he had really gotten into acid and had started tripping almost every other day.

Even the most ardent psychedelics enthusiast does not often trip more than once a week, usually only about two or three times a month. Taken at the dosage which Bill described, acid does not so much provide explorations of inner feelings as successfully block out the surrounding environment.

When Ed asked about his family, Bill quickly responded that his father had been a great guy and that he liked his three younger sisters. But he would not comment on his mother, even when questioned directly. The next day, however, Bill waited for Ed to come and then asked to speak to him outside. In a voice that sounded like it was making a confession, Bill said that he had been unable to please his mother and consequently had gotten along miserably with her over the past three years. Lowering his head, he said he was not sure why. When Ed finally asked what had happened between Bill and his mother to cause the rupture, Bill looked deeply embarrassed and took a very long time to answer. In a halting voice, he finally told Ed that he had run out of his father's funeral because he "just couldn't take it." His mother became furious, yelling that his bolting the funeral home showed that he had no respect or love for his father. He added that all his relatives and parents' friends had kept telling him that he had to be the man of the family and be strong to help his mother and sisters.

The youth had become deeply resentful, but he had not shown it because he felt that they only told him this so they could feel less guilty about not helping his family. After this Bill did not remain long in school, feeling both too upset to study even the small amount necessary to pass and too guilty over not working and contributing at home. After working for a year and then being laid off, Bill tried to find another job, though his mother accused him of being both lazy and irresponsible. The youth said that he finally split from home because his mother was driving him crazy by nagging and being unsatisfied no matter how hard he tried. Bill had lived with friends and on the streets for the previous year, communicating with his mother only through his sisters.

During the next month that Bill was at the storefront, he withdrew from the circle of kids there. Although he could still talk to Ed, he became quieter and developed some frightening catatonic symptoms. At first no one knew why this was happening, except that all the acid he had taken was perhaps catching up with him. Ed eventually learned that Bill had witnessed two guys starting a fight on the Common. He had attempted to intervene but failed; not only did he get shoved around quite a bit, but he also saw one of the combatants get so seriously beaten up that onlookers had to take him to the hospital. All this violence had made him intensely upset, and his withdrawal started the next day. Ed did not think this was the sole cause of Bill's present behavior, but he did believe that it triggered what followed. Sometimes he would strike up mechanistic body poses, as if he were a robot, for long periods of time. His face occasionally lapsed into contorted expressions that seemed to last for too long. He was never violent. Bill seemed unaware of what he was doing with his body; he would simply sit and stare.

Immediately the counselors decided something had to be done; the other kids in the storefront were becoming quite alarmed over Bill's welfare. Ed called Bill's home and made an appointment for Bill at a mental hospital in

Boston. When Mrs. Andrews came in to look at her son at the storefront, she could not believe his condition and kept murmuring, "I never knew, I never knew." That afternoon the staff arranged for his commitment.

Some counselors felt sure that this was the correct action since Sanctuary was simply not giving Bill the help he obviously needed. Others disagreed, saying that to get into a home or commune which offered trust and real connections with other people was what he really needed and would not be able to find in a state hospital. When Ed went to see Bill a week later, he found him standing in a corner, faced inward. When Ed called to him, Bill turned around and ran to him, crying. After that visit, Ed, for one, was sure that Bill was simply being ignored in the hospital for most of the time, while at Sanctuary "at least there were people who tried to talk with him, who cared for him, and tried to connect with him, no matter how difficult."

The entire question of handling disturbed people becomes even more difficult when the counselor must make a decsion after being with the strangely acting young person for only a very short time, say a couple of hours. She has no way of knowing whether the problem is confined to that particular point in time and space, whether the person has perhaps just experienced something that would have made anyone act "crazy," if only for a while, or whether the person may simply be having a terrible trip induced by a psychedelic drug or some substance sold as such a drug or be suffering the after-effects of a trip.

David

The case of David Lippman, a twenty-five-year-old high school teacher, raised several tricky ethical and practical questions. Helen and Peter, close friends of David's, brought him to the storefront one Sunday night in September to ask for some advice. They told Ellen, the counselor on duty, that after David had spent the summer at home with his parents, he had returned to Boston in a "completely flipped out" condition. When he was depressed earlier in the evening, he had called his parents in Maine; they detected that David was in bad shape and assured him that they would come get him early Monday morning. When he realized what he had done, he became terrified of seeing his parents at that time. The friends were very concerned that David not be sent home if home was, as they suspected, the source of many of his problems.

Helen and Peter were trying to figure out if they had the right to keep David away from his parents, the possibility of any legal problem, and where they could find a sympathetic psychiatrist to treat David. Ellen was moved by the care and love the couple showered on David and believed that they were asking excellent questions.

The trio stayed at Sanctuary for a short time. David was of average height, handsome in a puckish way with wavy brown hair and large brown eyes. He moved around constantly, singing limericks, poems, and snatches from Beatle songs; occasionally he would dash into the traffic, only to be restrained by Peter. Someone suggested that Ellen and the others take him to the city hospital, but once they got in the car they all just sat and thought while David spouted madly in the background. Although it was past midnight they called a psychiatrist, a friend of a friend of Ellen's who lived in a local commune; the doctor agreed to see David, so they quickly drove over.

When they arrived, the doctor seemed to calm David down considerably. Ten minutes after the doctor returned upstairs, however, David let loose again, ripping his clothes, running around outside, singing. About an hour later the psychiatrist came downstairs again, talked to David, and calmed him down. The doctor then spoke to Ellen and David's friends about taking care of people who were as freaked out as David was that night. Ellen says now that the comments gave her a whole new view of crisis counseling. According to Ellen, the doctor said that any attempt to figure out David's "head" would be very unwise at that point and that a lot of questions would further confuse him. David was all wound up inside and needed to do a lot of unwinding. It would only be egotistical to try to figure him out now in order to discuss him; and no counselor could really be on his trip with him. David needed a stable environment with people around who respected him a lot and would provide affection. The doctor explained that many crazy people are not in hospitals because they have relatives or friends to "babysit" for them. Those who have no one to babysit for them end up in institutions. Only after a long period of babysitting could therapy begin.

The next morning, after Ellen, Helen, Peter, and David had spent the night together, they drove to David's apartment, where they found his parents already waiting. They seemed calm, but the father was anxious that David's neighbors would notice the commotion and wanted to leave. Ellen asked herself if this rather elderly and stiff couple could create the warm, stable environment that David needed. Faced with the physical presence of David's parents, Ellen felt that to keep David separate from them seemed totally impossible to manage, even if it were sorely needed. David became tense and was now holding in, with effort, all the energy and dancing that he had furiously expressed before. The Lippmans collected their son and were gone only twenty minutes after Ellen had arrived.

Two weeks later, Ellen ran into Peter, who said that David's condition had deteriorated while he was home and that his parents had committed him to a nearby mental hospital. Peter had not even been able to talk to David; he added that he had not before informed Ellen of what had happened because he thought it would make her "too depressed." At this point Ellen regretted not seriously considering any way to prevent David from returning to his home situation.

David's case is instructive. Even though Ellen felt that she had not done enough, her action on the night of his crisis was considerable. Many people, faced with such a situation, would turn to a psychiatrist immediately—any psychiatrist. That Helen and Peter were wary of psychiatrists is justifiable; an evaluation at a hospital usually proceeds along set lines. Doctors have standard procedures for judging a person's "sense of reality," "intellectual functioning," and "level of affect," all of which may have little to do with the inner reality which a person is experiencing at the moment. These procedures have been developed to help a psychiatrist reach quick conclusions about a patient's mental state so that she may decide whether or not a patient should be committed to a hospital. These criteria were invented so that doctors could deal rapidly and efficiently with large numbers of diverse individuals; it is our opinion, however, that these criteria are not only insensitive but may also be misleading. In several of Sanctuary's cases, psychiatrists have, again in our opinion, used the power of involuntary commitment in an unjust, or at least a far too hasty, fashion. When a counselor took a young man named Alan to a local clinic for a prearranged interview with one clinician, another psychiatrist, visiting from another hospital, insisted on doing the evaluation. After *only ten minutes,* the psychiatrist told Alan that he was going to be sent to a mental hospital and began filling out commitment papers. Although Alan had acted strangely with the Sanctuary staff, laughing and talking incessantly, he became serious and attentive when faced with the prospect of commitment. He insisted that he would not go to the mental hospital; the psychiatrist paternalistically replied that the youth *would* go and continued with the form. Alan asked, "Then you're forcing me to go?" The doctor responded with, "You might say that." Sanctuary counselors and clinic personnel, however, insisted that Alan be interviewed by somone else; only this kept the psychiatrist from completing the form.

Because of such incidents, Ellen's belief that an official, clinical psychiatric evaluation might not be the best course of action appears prudent. By turning to someone who would try to help David with his immediate problem rather than exercise authority over what should be "done" with him, she was able to find an alternative to the only route open to most "crazy" people. If someone is judged mentally ill in the original interview, she is committed to a mental hospital for a brief period of observation–for either ten or thirty days–and then hospital psychiatrists make a more permanent decision. Yet even if the period were one night it would be unfair. The doctor's sympathetic treatment brought David aid he probably would not have found in the emergency room of a big city hospital or on the ward of a state asylum. The problems raised by these and other cases have made staff members concerned about alternative ways of caring for disturbed young people.

Despite all our misgivings about mental hospitals, Sanctuary sometimes acts in direct cooperation with them when it appears that this is the best line of action for the individual involved. In cases where the young people clearly might harm others or themselves, Sanctuary has had no recourse except to try to get them into a mental hospital. Occasionally, Sanctuary handles cases where the individuals simply need a rest from the street, almost a recuperation period: this is especially useful for the few individuals addicted or habituated to drugs who want to dry out, but do not trust themselves to do it on the outside.

MADNESS AND THE STREETS

In *The Pursuit of Loneliness,* Philip Slater quite correctly states that America's "ideas about institutionalizing the aged, psychotic, retarded, and infirm are based on a pattern of thought that we might call the Toilet Assumption–the notion that unwanted matter, unwanted difficulties, unwanted complexities, and obstacles will disappear if they are removed from our immediate field of vision. . . We throw the aged and psychotic into institutional holes where they cannot be seen. Our approach to social problems is to decrease their visibility: out of sight, out of mind" (p. 15). By incarcerating disturbed street people in mental hospitals, society does spare itself not only the bother they cause, but also the need to become conscious of the collective failure which these young people often represent. It is not hard to speculate upon how the specific nature of mental hospitals and prevailing psychiatric attitudes are part and parcel of this "Toilet Assumption."

Because they cannot accept the idea that "crazy" people belong out of the way, the Sanctuary staff must deal daily with problems most people choose not to recognize. A local psychiatrist informed us that the Sanctuary had a reputation in the community for concentrating on pathological cases. He warned the counselors that many people were skeptical about the kind of counseling done at the Sanctuary and reported that some professionals thought that the counselors were as pathological as the kids. Such statements are but another example of how psychological language can be used as a way of invalidating human experience. Since the staff refuses to employ conventional labels and standards used to pigeonhole the young people they work with, they are conscious that, perhaps even more than others, they work in the dark. The counselors, like the street people, give what they have and do what they can. If an outside chance exists that an emotionally conflicted young person "will make it" despite his problems, the staff fights for that chance, even if it means struggling hard against the young person's self-destructive or defeatist impulses. In such instances the counselors as well as the kids are often rebelling against society's definition of who is normal. It is possible that, if careless, the counselors might go too far, especially in permitting people to stay on the streets where they may harm themselves or others or in aiding them to avoid mental hospitals where, allegedly, they might "get the help they needed." This danger is lessened by the fact that the advice of sympathetic psychiatrists is solicited and followed wherever possible.

Nico

Nico Dean, a tall, twenty-one-year-old girl from Lowell, was unable to survive in her parents' home and would probably have been committed, if she had not escaped to live on the streets. Alice, Nico's counselor, describes her as "incredibly spaced out," and always "just wandering around with one or two men following her." Nico had taken dozens of acid trips over the previous year. When she first came into the storefront, she wore very brief, tight shorts with a thin silver halter. She had little will in either the trivial or the crucial areas of her life. When she was permitted to help distribute food in the hostel, which she had asked to do, she helped exactly one person get food and then split, leaving the job unattended. Nico had started three different jobs, including one as a bartender in a club, but she always quit within the week. At different times she told several boys that she "loved" them, and then the next night appeared with another man in tow, badly wounding and embarrassing her previous "love." Finally, and most important from Nico's viewpoint since it made her miserable, at many times she had no will in sexual matters; men often took advantage of her. What is deviant in a home environment can become less noticeable or more defensible by the nature of living on the streets. In Nico's case, her sexual activity, considered delinquent at home, became functional on the streets: both men and women exchange sex for a bed and food for a night.

Nico had left home two years before, when her parents threatened to put her away if she would not stop her escapades, mostly sexual, with men. Since she left, they have disowned her. During the summer, Nico's older sister called her at Sanctuary every week, and, by the fall, Nico had gone to live with this sister, with whom she got along fairly well. Though not perfectly happy while she lived on the streets and hung around at Sanctuary, she did have people who were warm, caring, and honest with her. Alice did not spare Nico's feelings, for example, about the issue of her running away from the job she had asked for, nor about the way she bruised the feelings of the men in the hostel who had liked her and not exploited her (as opposed to those who had wanted to exploit her). Despite the fact that Nico herself had said that she did not "like women," she did manage to form a close friendship with another girl, though there were many arguments between them at first.

When Nico complained about her inability to refuse men when they wanted to sleep with her, Alice tried, in as warm and responsive a way as she could, to point out two things: first, that some other women slept with as many men as Nico did, and this was not cause for her to think that she was worthless; this was important because this feeling then led her to sleep with more men to prove that she was desirable; second, that Nico could exercise a little more control, could remember not to get herself in positions where either she or the man would think it incumbent upon her to sleep with him. Over the summer, Nico became somewhat less promiscuous, which made her feel better, although she felt guilt whenever she "lapsed." By the fall, Alice and Nico agreed that Nico might be better off at her sister's home. Although Alice cannot be totally impartial, since she was deeply involved in the case, she strongly believes that Nico is now better off for having lived on the streets than if she had been committed to a mental hospital.

Craig

Sometimes the counselors really had to struggle to prevent a young person from being committed. Craig Rich, a seventeen-year-old black youth from Roxbury is a prime example of this kind of occurrence. Craig was just over six feet tall, weighed more than 175 pounds, and had one of the biggest Afro hairdos the staff had seen. He arrived wearing jeans, no shirt, many strings of beads, and sandals. Although he seemed unsophisticated, he was shrewd in some ways: in his first encounter with Sanctuary, he was able to talk his way into staying at the hostel when admissions had been closed. Later that day he talked to Tom, who wrote that "Craig is very depressed, expressed threats of suicide. Seems he can't find a job or an apartment, which distresses him. Claims he needs to see Dr. Gold (his psychiatrist at a Boston hospital) 'a hell-of-a-lot more' than the once-a-week Dr. Gold offers."

Tom reports that Craig was "incredibly difficult." The boy was loud and boisterous and demanded an enormous amount of attention from the staff in ways which Tom described as "highly creative." Craig especially played up to the women counselors, "acting as a child to get a kind of maternal response which he could turn into a sexual fantasy," according to Tom. On one hand, the counselors cared a great deal about Craig and felt they should chase him each and every time he did something dramatically self-destructive, like running out into the traffic in front of the hostel. On the other, they believed that he would not actually commit suicide, but was instead making them play his games in a bid for attention. The counselors were unsure how they could avoid seeming to neglect Craig and yet put limits on the attention they gave him so that they could still respond to the other kids.

Craig's inability to manage on a worldly level astounded Tom through his stay at Sanctuary. Craig was trying to save the little money he had until his social worker could get him some welfare money to live on. But he could not add well and never knew if people were giving him the right change. He also never could account for where he spent his money. Once he gave away all the money he had left "just to make some friends." At another point, he and a new friend were going to take a hike into the country; so Craig spent a lot of money to buy a generous amount of food for the two for the trip, only to have the other boy, who was probably hungry, rip off all the food and disappear. Craig felt helpless, at the mercy of thieves, which he really was. He simply could not understand injustice and the manifestations of selfishness and unfairness which are present, perhaps in a small way, in all human interchanges. In many ways his relations with other people were really out of control despite his efforts at making friends and demanding attention from helping agencies.

About four days later, after asking Craig's permission, Tom contacted his social worker, who provided more background about Craig. The social worker confirmed

Tom's belief that Craig was not suicidal and that the counselors did not have to watch him so closely. Tom knew a little of Craig's family background, but the social worker helped him put it all together. Craig's mother had deserted his father when the boy was eight. Craig and Mr. Rich lived alone for a couple of years, till the father remarried a woman with whom Craig did not get along at all. When Craig was twelve, the father died, and the stepmother did not want to keep him (and probably could not have controlled him if she had). The boy then lived in two orphanages (few foster homes are available for black kids), finally ran away, was picked up and committed to a mental hospital, where he stayed for two and a half years.

During his last year there he had begun to see Dr. Gold, to whom he was greatly attached. The doctor tried to get the boy out of the hospital into a school where he might have a chance. He was at that time formally released from the hospital, but he ran away anyway, apparently trying to forestall going to the school. Since then, about six months before the boy came to Sanctuary, he had been knocking around, traveling from place to place. The social worker stated that the staff should encourage Craig to go see Dr. Gold again. He concluded that we should keep him as long as we could, but if he became impossible to control, the social worker would try to get Craig into a state hospital.

Tom had already decided that Craig needed a supportive group or person and a protected job. After his talk with the social worker, he felt that Dr. Gold was the best person to try to work things out with Craig. Since Craig had already expressed anger at the doctor, Tom thought a simple suggestion would not be very effective. He tried to get Craig to talk about his feelings toward Dr. Gold. (It was up to Craig to start the relationship again.) It became clear that Craig felt extremely abandoned and betrayed by Dr. Gold because of what seemed to be the limits of his professional capacity. Craig felt that Dr. Gold did not care for him because he had tried to "send him away" and because he would not see him more than once a week. Besides wanting more attention, which, to a love-starved person resembles love, he also wanted to feel that he mattered to Dr. Gold and was not just a patient, but also someone to whom the doctor liked to talk.

Tom learned that Dr. Gold was really the only significant person in Craig's world who was gentle and caring to the boy, and Craig wanted a lot from him. Tom tried to make Craig see that the doctor had done all he possibly could, that it was a general rule that psychiatrists only saw their patients once a week, and that Dr. Gold really did respect Craig: didn't Dr. Gold think enough of Craig to try to get him out of the hospital? After a great deal of inspired argumentation on Tom's part, the counselors pushed Craig to make an appointment with Dr. Gold and then pushed him to keep it. In a way, Tom used Craig's friendship with the counselors and other kids as a threat: he said that Craig could stay with Sanctuary only if he tried to make his situation better by reestablishing contact with Dr. Gold.

Tom said that the only way out for Craig was to give up the idea of being a street kid and seriously consider therapy with Dr. Gold. Tom met Craig at the storefront a few days later and drove him to the hospital, where Craig tried to get Tom to accompany him inside on the grounds that they would commit him as soon as they saw him. Tom argued that this was not the case, knowing that Craig understood this to be false and only wanted an excuse to ask Tom to come along. After the session, Dr. Gold said that the meeting had been worthwhile and that Craig really seemed intent on improving his life. Dr. Gold and the social worker then proceeded to try and get Craig on welfare so that he could get an apartment. Till that money came, Dr. Gold asked the counselors to keep Craig in the hostel as long as he behaved himself. The doctor told Tom not to hesitate to confront Craig if he was being too loud, too demanding of attention. The doctor added that Craig could be asked to take some responsibility for the situation.

Clearly, Nico and Craig needed help. Yet, let us look briefly at the manifestations of their conflicts that would have motivated other people to believe that they should be committed—that is, not the basic problem, but the behavior which would have prompted commitment. For the most part, although Nico had other problems as well, her parents were outraged over her sexual misconduct; they would have had her committed because she would not or was not able to obey the current social rules governing the interaction of twenty-year-old girls with men. The problem for her was that she could control her sexual activity so little that it made her feel guilty and worthless. Craig was first admitted to the mental hospital because he was unable to play the game of being happy in an orphanage, of accepting just a small fraction of the care and attention that children want from their parents. If the Sanctuary counselors had decided that he was indeed too much trouble to look after, he might have been committed for failing to remember not to cause people powerful in his life (since the counselors could have recommended commitment) too much effort or bother.

Nico and Craig both ran afoul of convention—and were hospitalized, or almost hospitalized, for it—but they defied convention out of deep, personal needs that had to be met. Nico and Craig survived on the streets because they found people who would take their current needs seriously rather than dismiss their behavior as a sign of mental illness. Three years after leaving home, the effect of parental influence still contributed to Nico's lack of self-esteem. At home her parents regularly told her that she was mad. With Alice, at least she had the chance to talk about the problems she was facing in everyday life. If she had been hospitalized, all the decisions about her life would have been in the hands of other people. On the streets, the problem of responsibility remained a real one for Nico. Craig also wanted a chance on the outside to do something for himself. Outside the hospital, Craig had a chance—even if only a slim one—to more actively seek the relationships he so sorely needed but simultaneously feared. As an out-patient he could begin to deal with his problems in the context of his daily life. If he were hospitalized, this would be impossible.

THERAPEUTIC COMMUNES

When an emotionally conflicted, alienated, inarticulate, and frightened working-class girl, picked up because she broke the law, is forced to be interviewed by a highly educated, establishment-oriented, middle-class doctor, it is natural to suspect that the doctor will believe the girl is "out of contact with reality." The girl *is* out of contact with the doctor's reality, and the doctor might seem similarly disconnected in the girl's situation of broken homes, poverty, and the streets.

They live in different worlds; they often have conflicting values concerning what is sane and what is not. The psychiatrist has never been really hungry, never without a comfortable home; her parents were probably never brutal to her; she is successful and probably respected. The young person has often been hungry, both before and since she left her home; no one has ever been sarcastic enough to call her a "success." And while the psychiatrist has probably been, on the whole, well-treated by groups and institutions, the poor, misbehaving young person has most likely been very poorly treated by institutions, such as her family, her school, the police, and the hospital in which she is now forcibly a patient.

The young person's drug use becomes a symptom of bizarre and inappropriate behavior. Statements of political opinions become symptoms of madness: if a young person admits that whenever she sees a policeman, she becomes very angry, calls him a "pig," and wants to throw a rock at him, this means that she is very unstable and cannot deal with authority. This might well be a good inference from the statement, but it overlooks something: the girl may have some justification for her feelings, since it is possible that police have mistreated her in the past. In many ways the cards are stacked against the doctor and the girl making contact: in fact, such confrontations are often, quite simply, disasters, leading to the commitment of the young person.

That Sanctuary counselors at least speak the "same language" as street kids greatly facilitates their ability to deal with them. A counselor can sympathize greatly, for example, with a kid's statement that the atrocities in Vietnam make her so angry that she must do something about it, even if the counselor strongly disagrees with the individual's method of expressing her outrage. Although the counselor may decide that other factors are influencing the young person's militant actions, the counselor does not feel that if only the person had no other conflicts, she would not be angry about the war in Vietnam.

Finally, we feel that mental hospitals, and many therapists in general, do harm by making the individuals they treat feel as if the problems they are struggling with are purely personal ones. In the above example, a therapist would probably try to figure out why the young person is feeling such conflict so intensely on this issue, implying that if the girl were not "ill" she would not feel so strongly about it. If a street girl, or any woman, for that matter, complains to a therapist that the men in her life exploit her, the therapist may support her in the sense of agreeing that she is indeed exploited, and may even help her plot out a strategy that will prevent such misuse in the future; but instead of making her see how her problems result from and are inseparable from society's patterns of exploiting women, the therapist will probably imply that the matter (and the fault) is personal: had she been more intelligent in planning her life, she would not be in such a mess.

Since we are not dealing with phenomena which can be viewed in an objective way, such as how well a person's heart functions, it is necessary to examine the viewpoint of the individuals who have the final power to say who is sane and who is not. From the comfortable, middle-class point of view of a physician, the psychiatrist attempts to evaluate behavior which can, in fact, be judged only from the point of view of the individual's peer group. Committing an individual on an involuntary basis partly reflects the fact that his behavior was very troublesome to a certain other person or group of persons. Commitment, therefore, becomes a political act, despite all disclaimers, since the commitment has been brought about by the wishes of a certain group, rather than for the overall good of the community, as would be the case with lepers, for example. Two yardsticks which psychiatrists use to determine whether or not an individual is "ill" are whether or not she is "out of contact with reality" or manifesting "inappropriate behavior." It seems logical and refreshing to ask "who determines reality?" and "inappropriate to what?"

As more people begin to ask these questions, new, truly therapeutic anti-institutions will be formed. The acceptance of mental hospitals is being challenged on several fronts. The pioneering work of R. D. Laing, which attempts to make madness comprehensible on the basis of the social context of a person's life, has already inspired the founding of new therapeutic communities in England as well as in America. Furthermore, laws governing commitment to mental hospitals are now being challenged in American courts. A recent decision by the Federal District Court of Pennsylvania ruled that those patients committed by a doctor's recommendation had been denied due process under the Constitution and should be freed. The decision involved over fourteen thousand persons held in ten state hospitals. Despite the judicial ruling, state mental health officials were making plans to keep most of the patients in the hospitals on a voluntary basis by getting consent of the family or the patient himself to continue hospitalization *(New York Times,* July 10, 1971, "Mental Patients Freed by Ruling"). It is possible, however, that the court challenge will force a change in commitment procedures so that a "crazy" person will have the same right to counsel when being interviewed by a psychiatrist as a suspect has when questioned by a police officer.

Changes in the law would make it more difficult for people to be committed unjustly, but a change in the treatment of "crazy" people is also badly needed. Since the standard ways of dealing with these people have proven so unsuccessful in the past, new ways must be developed. It is in the spirit of looking for new forms of treatment that the following ideal model of a therapeutic community is put forward.

The basic assumption behind a therapeutic community is that it must be geared to the needs of its members. The organization and staffing should be planned around truly therapeutic ends, not in accordance with any predetermined institutional models which society finds it difficult to reject despite ample evidence of their failure.

The commune need not be based fundamentally on a distinction between crazy patients and sane doctors. Such a distinction locks both patients and doctors into fixed roles that limit their capacity for growth, and presupposes that patients should be made to conform to what the society calls sane. A preferable attitude would be to assume that every member of the community is already a unique and good person who might want to explore in full depth her experience of the inner and outer worlds in the hope of realizing as much of her potential as possible. In this way all the members could try to learn from each other about the whole range of the human condition.

Inevitably, kids and psychiatrists will have had vastly different experiences, and their perceptions of people and situations will vary greatly. If they can share these perceptions in an open and meaningful way their understanding of each other, and therefore their capacity to help, will be deepened. No one should be anyone else's patient unless she chooses to be. Counseling and therapy should not be compulsory, but individual and group therapy should be available on both an occasional and an intensive basis. Specialists trained in dealing with the varieties of madness, psychiatrists as well as qualified laymen, should be present, however, so that the others would feel secure enough to misbehave or "sink down" into their own madness. It is crucial that there should be the space, freedom, and support required for people to act in ways society defines as mad if they feel they must. This kind of support for madness should include concrete help in working through conflicts when the person feels ready to do so, as well as a general tolerance of eccentric behavior. A truly supportive environment would be one in which no negative assumptions were made about madness and in which people tried to respond to each other and themselves in honest and direct ways, instead of ignoring behavior which they considered fearful. Such a community should serve as an alternative to mental institutions and to the family as a therapeutic supportive group. Ways must be found to integrate these roles. Traditionally institutions have stepped into custodial roles when families have failed as supportive groups, whereas the therapeutic communities we envisage would hopefully provide both care and support.

In mental institutions doctors and staff often refuse or neglect to treat patients as fully human; patients are therefore unable to view the authorities as human beings. For this reason, we feel that despite some inequality between a severely upset patient and a more stable counselor, members of the community should be free to relate to any other member as an equal: to expect things from them, to disagree with them, to touch them, and to love them. Members should be encouraged to help in the care and transformation of fellow members. Struggling to survive and grow together offers much of the therapeutic promise of the anti-institutions. Mutual trust and openness should not receive only lip service, but should be considered a goal worth struggling toward.

Depending on their capabilities members should have real responsibilities which they would be expected by all to live up to, especially when those responsibilities involve the needs of others. For example, if the assigned members fail to prepare dinner, other members should be permitted to be appropriately angry with them for this lapse.

The members of these communities must become as free as possible from dependence on typical forms of restraint or coercion. In the context of an open and supportive group in which "madness" is permissible, it seems possible to enable members to be free from needing tranquilizers to survive or supervisors to tell them what to do. Clearly, however, it might be necessary for some people to be restrained from harming themselves or others.

With mental patients, their initial and binding commitment to the hospital is a very important form of coercion. Young people especially are often committed involuntarily by the decision of their parents and a doctor;

once in the institution they can only leave with a psychiatrist's approval. Ideally, membership in a therapeutic community would be voluntary. We realize, however, that for the present, young people will continue to be committed to institutions and therefore feel that it would be advisable to encourage parents and psychiatrists who have control over young people's lives to think of commitment to a therapeutic community as a viable alternative to established institutions.

Who will be the members of these communities? Their ages and characteristics will obviously vary greatly from one community to another. Some existing halfway houses for mental hospitals have been changing their original criteria for membership. They no longer accept only ex-mental-patients, but are including young people who are experiencing many different conflicts and difficulties in living. We hope that therapeutic communities will maintain as much flexibility as possible in accepting members and forming a group which can meet its own needs.

Both the ages of the individuals and the severity of the conflicts they are experiencing would determine the kind of staff that could best help make the group as therapeutically effective as possible. For a group composed primarily of younger kids, it might be desirable to have a larger number of elders who could work closely with them in adjusting to their new living situation and responsibilities. For a group in which many of the members had severe conflicts to work through, it would be necessary to have staff available who had considerable experience in counseling and could form intensive therapeutic relationships with the other members. In all situations there should be a considerable range in age, as well as enough members so that many of the community's needs could be satisfied by the members themselves, increasing the group's sense of autonomy and worth.

Important for all, and especially younger members, would be opportunities for them to become interested in something outside themselves, in some skill or activity. We hope that in the context of the therapeutic community opportunities for learning would seem exciting and inspirational. The skills taught and classes offered would probably differ markedly from the rigid and confining structures of education in many schools, from many parents' expectations of what their kids should learn, and from the traditional kinds of occupational therapy provided in many of the "good" mental hospitals. A free school, libraries, yoga classes, painting studios—all these would be appropriate. If such a community is to play more than a socializing role in the lives of its members, then whatever is taught and learned should grow out of the particular interests and talents of its members and should not be imposed according to some external imperative. To make learning an integral part of the group's daily life, the possibility of experimenting with artists in residence might also be considered. The members themselves should be encouraged to share their own interests and talents—contemporary literature or weaving, for example—with each other. It seems crucial to encourage in whatever imaginative ways possible members to learn a skill or develop a talent which would help them express themselves and be independent, and in which they could take pride.

The older members of the community as well as the kids themselves should help each other relate their conflicts to the family or society in which the problems began. Whenever possible, members might consider ways in which they could modify the society which set the scene of their conflicts. The members should also become thoroughly aware of the undeniable fact that no matter what "caused" their madness, they and they alone are, in the final analysis, responsible for their own lives and should plan and act accordingly.

BIBLIOGRAPHY

Erikson, Erik H. *Childhood and Society*. New York: W. W. Norton, 1964.

Goffman, Erving. *Asylums: Essays on the Social Situation of Mental Patients and Other Inmates.* Garden City, N.Y.: Doubleday, 1961.

Goodman, Paul. *Growing Up Absurd.* New York: Random House, 1960.

Grier, William H., and Price M. Cobbs. *Black Rage.* New York: Bantam Books, 1969.

Laing. R. D. "In Search of a New Psychiatry." *The Atlantic* 227 (January 1971): 50-53.

——— *The Politics of Experience.* New York: Ballantine Books, 1971.

——— A. Esterson, *Sanity, Madness, and the Family: Families of Schizophrenics.* Baltimore, Md.: Pelican Books, 1970.

Marin, Peter, and Allan Y. Cohen. *Understanding Drug Use: An Adult's Guide to Drugs and the Young.* New York: Harper and Row, 1971.

Slater, Philip. *The Pursuit of Loneliness: American Culture at the Breaking Point.* Boston, Mass.: Beacon Press, 1970.

Szasz, Thomas S., *Ideology and Insanity: Essays on the Psychiatric Dehumanization of Man.* Garden City, N.Y.: Doubleday, 1970.

DATE DUE

MAR 10 '75	MAR 10 '75		
NOV 21 '75	NOV 17 '75		
MR 03 '86	MAR 3 '86		
AP 27 '89	MAY 5 '89		